THE LOVER
AND THE BELOVED

JOHN MICHAEL TALBOT

The
LOVER
and the
BELOVED

A Way of
Franciscan Prayer

✣ ✣ ✣

CROSSROAD · NEW YORK

1991
The Crossroad Publishing Company
370 Lexington Avenue, New York, N.Y. 10017

Library of Congress Cataloging in Publication Data

Talbot, John Michael.
The lover and the beloved.

Bibliography: p. 123.
1. Prayer. 2. God—love. 3. God—Worship and love.
4. Franciscans—Spiritual life. 5. Spiritual life—
Catholic authors. I. Title.
BV215.T28 1985   248.3'2   85-17110
ISBN 0-8245-0717-7

CONTENTS

ACKNOWLEDGMENTS

Writing a book about prayer can be a very active experience. Oh, it starts prayerfully enough ... sitting peacefully at my hermitage desk, looking out across our little mountain lake, jotting down ideas that drift through my morning meditations, or writing down a quote from a spiritual master that I found inspiring and helpful. Soon a large and bulky manuscript is amassed, sitting on my desk like a weight of burdensome human thoughts where once my spirit prayed a sacred hymn into the realms of divinity as if it were lighter than air.

It took the help of one special person to prune this manuscript back to a healthy and fruitful vine. I would like to thank that expert "husbandman" Michael Leach for his editorial pruning; he snipped a limb here and a limb there with love, kindness, and concern.

Now that I have submitted the final draft to the publisher, I can once again sit in my quiet hermitage without the nuisance of having to write down my thoughts. They can again be prayer. But knowing God, more books will come from this prayer. I can't win for losing, but it is only in losing that we will find.

INTRODUCTION

In the course of my life as a Franciscan and as a Christian musician, many people have asked me to write a book on Franciscan prayer. These requests come from my Franciscan brothers and sisters and even more so from men and women who are interested in knowing the sources behind my musical prayer and workshops on prayer. This book is an attempt to respond to that need.

Curiously, even after 800 years, it remains very difficult to describe the prayer life of Franciscans and especially of St. Francis! While many other great monastic figures of the East and West, as well as the great Carmelite and Dominican mystics, have left us orderly, detailed accounts of their mystical prayer, Francis was content to leave us simply his example. His personal prayer life defies any attempt to box it within a method, and no early biographer ever attempted to synthesize his mystical prayer. Instead, the writer had to snatch it from the quaint stories of the first brothers, or pull it from the lines, even from between the lines, of Francis's few personal writings. Even then, the biographer could only reinforce the fact that Francis was so rapt in the mystical love of Jesus that his prayer could not be frozen in human words.

It is only with St. Bonaventure (1218–1274), the successor to Francis, that we begin to see an endeavor to describe the mystical life of all Christians from a "Franciscan" perspective. And even then, Bonaventure rarely dares to describe the "deep waters" of Francis's prayer. Bonaventure instead focuses on the mystical life from his own perspective as a Franciscan. In this he is extremely successful, combining his own keen intellect with the simple mystical rapture of Francis into a synthesis of divine love that won for him the title of "Seraphic Doctor."

From the time of Bonaventure in the thirteenth century came other efforts to describe the mystical life within the Franciscan tradition. While writing has always taken a back seat to popular teaching in the apostolic life of Franciscans, nonetheless some wonderful works on mystical prayer have been brought forth by Franciscan writers.

One such work is *The Book of the Lover and the Beloved* by the thirteenth-century Franciscan hermit, Blessed Ramon Lull (1232–1316), who has done much to inspire me in my life as a hermit and troubadour. Ramon lived for many years as a hermit on Mt. Randa in Italy. During that time, he developed many mystical and theological works designed to explain Jesus Christ to Moslems. As a result, this itinerant hermit-preacher has often been called the founder of the Franciscan missionary movement. Yet at the heart of his mysticism rests a simple understanding of his personal love relationship with Jesus Christ that is best expressed in the above-mentioned work, an understanding which I have found to ring true in my own prayer experience.

In this book I hope to describe mystical prayer as I, too, have experienced it, in terms of the intimate relationship between a man and a woman, or the Lover and the Beloved. This, to me, is an important part of the core of Franciscan spirituality and the focus of this presentation. I do not pretend to offer a comprehensive study of Franciscan prayer but rather a summary of the essentials, using many of the Franciscan sources available in English, so that the reader, if he or she wishes, can go to some of these marvelous texts for deeper appreciation of certain stages of the mystical life from this unique perspective. As Francis of Assisi sought to make the gospel of Jesus Christ the beginning and end of the Franciscan life, so I pray this book will serve no other end than fostering a personal love relationship with Jesus within all who read it, that all may begin to know the mystical love union that occurs between the Lover and the Beloved.

1

THE BRIDE AND THE GROOM

Mystical prayer is a personal love relationship with Jesus Christ. Scripture encourages us to use the language of a bride and groom in describing this intimate relationship. As the great song of rejoicing in Revelation 19:6–8 says:

> *Let us rejoice and be glad*
> *and give him glory!*
> *For this is the wedding day*
> *of the Lamb;*
> *His Bride has prepared herself*
> *for the wedding.*
> *She has been given a dress to wear,*
> *made of the finest linen,*
> *brilliant white.*

(The linen dress is the virtuous deeds of God's saints.)

A wedding day is, indeed, an awesome event. It is a day of great rejoicing, expectation, and hope. Yet it is also a day of healthy fear and awe before the great challenges facing this courageous couple coming to join their lives as one.

Many times I have provided a special song or instrumental music at my friends' weddings. Each time I have meditated on the awesome spiritual mystery beginning that day, I found my knees growing weak, a lump rising in my throat, my mouth suddenly dry. Ironically, this so-called "professional" singer, author of many records, having performed world-wide for hundreds of thousands, finds it difficult to maintain his composure at a friend's wedding!

It is the same for me at both Catholic and Protestant weddings. I see the symbols that signify this mystical union between two people, think of the beautiful challenge of life ahead of them . . . and turn to emotional jelly. The bells and chimes blend in perfect harmony with the smiles and laughter of the people. Yet we all know there will be some tears ahead. The scriptures are read in solemnity, and words of encouragement are offered in homily or sermon. Still, the time will come when both bride and groom will be tempted to ignore flippantly the active word of God in their lives, as well as the Spirit-led discernment of their brothers and sisters. Two individual candles will be extinguished in self-sacrifice in order to light up the one bright flame of a larger candle, set high up on the altar. But one day, the flame of selfless love union will seem to burn dimly, even threatening to die out in the weakness of human pride and sin. Finally, one Bread of Life is broken so that these two precious souls may become truly one in the love of Christ. Yet we know that times of great brokenness await this now joyful and confident couple.

However, it is in this human brokenness that the bride and groom will be united and healed truly by the divine love of God. For what takes place on one day in sign, symbol, and sacrament will occur in personal experience time and time again in the years to come. In a seemingly endless cycle of deaths and resurrections, this couple will become one and, growing into full maturity in Christ, will give birth to much new life from the womb of brokenness and darkness. If this couple has the courage to "stick it out" through the tough times, they will look back one day to discover a relationship that has deepened and grown unshakably strong, as it blossoms like a tree in the divine mystery of human love. How true are the words of the sixteenth-century Carmelite mystic Teresa of Avila: "Patient endurance all things attaineth!"

It is no less true in our love relationship with Jesus. There are many signs, symbols, and sacraments associated with the "wedding day of our marriage" to Him, beginning with our baptism and culminating in our entrance into heaven. But the unfolding of that relationship through life involves many stages of growth. There will be joy and sorrow, excitement and boredom, light and darkness. At times we will feel impregnated and enlived by the very life of Jesus. But other times we will feel totally empty and abandoned by Him. Yet the wisdom of time will show that He has never once left us nor forsaken us.

For me, this is what Christian prayer really is . . . remaining faithful to Jesus "for better or worse, for richer or poorer, in sickness and in health," discovering that our mystical love union has grown deep and strong in the continual unfolding of this commitment to love. However, unlike a human marriage, death will not part us. Rather, it is the full experience of both the death and resurrection of Jesus that gives purpose to my solitude and makes joyful my intimate communion with Him.

The scriptures are full of references to this "bride and bridegroom" mysticism in describing the relationship between God and His people. Jesus Himself uses "knowing" Him (Mt. 7:23) as a condition for salvation, and it is significant that the word "know" is the same word used in the Old Testament to describe the sexual union between a man and a woman. Paul speaks of the relationship between the Church and Jesus as symbolized by the relationship between a wife and her husband (Eph. 5:22–27). He goes on to speak of himself as a father who has given the individuals and whole church at Corinth as a virgin daughter who takes Jesus as her Husband (2 Cor. 11:2). He also speaks of himself as a mother who has given birth to many spiritual babes in Christ (Gal. 4:19; 1 Cor. 3:1–2), showing how he personally applied his own teaching. Soon the early Church began to interpret the Old Testament references to the bride and bridegroom (Is. 5:1–7; 54:4–8; Jer. 2:32; Ezek. 16:23; Hos. 1–3) as referring to the relationship between Jesus and the Church. It was not long before the Song of Songs, complete with graphic sexual language, was used to describe this relationship.

From this scriptural basis the early Church fathers began to develop a primitive mystical theology using the analogy of the bride and groom to describe a personal love relationship with Jesus. By the eleventh century, St. Bernard of Clairvaux (1091–1153) will write a whole treatise on the passionate Song of Songs as an allegory of the Christian mystical life. In this work he writes in passionate terms about "the kiss of the mouth" we should seek from Jesus, our divine Lover. Finally, the great Carmelite reformer, St. John of the Cross (1542–1591), brought this approach to its summit in his poetry and mystical theology. His understanding of the relationship between the Lover and the Beloved is beautifully portrayed in this excerpt from "The Ascent of Mt. Carmel":

> *O night that has united*
> *the Lover with His Beloved,*
> *transforming the Beloved*
> *in her Lover.*
>
> *Upon my flowering breast*
> *which I kept wholly for Him alone,*
> *there He lay sleeping,*
> *and I caressing Him . . .*

Or one could look to his "Spiritual Canticle" to see a whole description of this relationship which could be said to rival the Song of Songs in beauty and doctrine.

However, when we read the works of the mystical greats we are often overwhelmed by the apparently complex spiritualities, full of "purgations," "illuminations," and "unifications." The language seems baffling, and the endless maze of scrupulous self-examinations and active or passive "dark nights" often take on the appearance of mere legalistic methods that differ in name only from the techniques of Far East non-Christian religions, or their Westernized counterparts.

Nonetheless, the mystical writers of Christianity have never lost sight of the central dimension of relationship with Jesus Christ. Though St. John of the Cross is a complex writer, the concept of the mystical bride and groom permeate his works from beginning to end, in a way that typifies Western Christian mysticism. And while the tradition of Eastern Christianity may be more trinitarian in its mysticism, the dimension of a relationship with Jesus, and in Jesus with the Trinity is always central to its vision and goal. As we will see, Franciscan mysticism brings about a full harmony of the East and West through a balanced emphasis on a personal love relationship with Jesus Christ, who leads us into a full experience of the Trinity.

Summary

A personal love relationship is not a static concept but a living reality. As such, there are stages of development that can be clearly discerned as the relationship matures. These stages are entered into by passing through them successively. First dialogue, then union and afterglow, followed by the joys and sorrows, losses and gains of daily life, transfused and transcended with the victorious cross of Christ. We need to know more about these stages before the relationship matures to ensure that it grows properly and without confusion. However, this should not be done in order to limit the love relationship, but to discipline and guide the relationship so that it might be fully fruitful.

Take the example of a fruit tree. There are certain stages through which a tree passes, and certain disciplines are applied to ensure its growth. Thus a tree is periodically pruned. If the tree is pruned at the wrong time it could kill the tree. On the other hand, when a tree is first pruned, it looks as if it is has nearly been killed, yet it will be twice as fruitful in the next season because it was pruned and not left to grow wild.

It is the same with a love relationship. Certain stages of growth and discipline are needed. Otherwise the relationship will grow wild and become virtually fruitless. The "womb of darkness" so necessary to nurturing love will instead be dry and barren. As Ramon Lull writes, "What is the greatest darkness? The absence of my Beloved. And what is the greatest light? The presence of my Beloved." But the awareness and study of these stages becomes a discipline in itself helping to ensure full life and fruitfulness in our personal love relationship with Jesus. Let's look at those stages and what they mean to us from a Franciscan perspective.

2
DIALOGUE

❧

The beginning of our love relationship with Christ can be likened to the first encounters between a man and a woman. An initial mystical spark occurs between them. Each is drawn to the other in a way that defies description. Granted, the external qualities of beauty and intelligence play their part, but beyond these is that mystical spark that marks one good-looking, intelligent person as more attractive than another. Both may have wonderful personalities, yet only one holds a romantic attraction. Nobody knows why this is so, just that it is part of the mystery of love.

And now the dialogue begins—establishing the facts, discerning the inner qualities of each other as well as the externals. Dialogue is the first stage in a genuine love relationship, for speech most effectively reveals the inner qualities of a person. "Out of the abundance of the heart a man speaks" (Lk. 6:45). At the beginning of the relationship, the couple will start to speak about what they want out of life, what they do not, what their goals are, and how they intend to achieve them. It is through dialogue that both initially come really to identify the true person to whom each is attracted.

We have all experienced the closeness that develops when

we dialogue in truth and love with one another. Be it friends or lovers, there comes that divinely magical moment in time when words are shared and the precious inner self is unveiled. It seems that time itself stands still during these "breakthrough" dialogues. One can't help but sense that these moments touch on the eternal and are an important part of our destiny. For even as the unveiling of the holy of holies was a sacred act in Jewish thought, so the unveiling of our inner self through dialogue is a revelation of mystery and holiness.

In Middle Eastern culture it is said that a person's word is the extension of his very soul. Consequently, spoken words are cherished as the precious jewels that make up the sacred crown of the human soul. So, in the stage of dialogue, each person shares in trust his or her deepest heart, and the other must cherish the spirit and truth of these words as a priceless and sacred jewel. How much more should we apply this truth to our relationship with Jesus who said, "My words are spirit and truth." Even greater than that, He is spoken of in scripture as the eternal Word of the Father. This is why He alone can and has permanently unveiled the holy of holies, revealing the deepest and most intimate mysteries of God.

But we, in the modern West, rarely speak or listen with the same awe and reverence which is common to our Middle Eastern brothers and sisters. For us, as the saying goes, "words are cheap." We throw them around easily in jest and idleness, making it very easy to break promises and forget oaths. For this same reason, we of the West talk much but communicate little. So we go to seminars and classes to learn how to "dialogue." Why? Because we no longer understand the sacred reality of the spoken word. We spend large sums of money to discover something as simple as the existence of the soul. It wouldn't hurt our bank accounts to remember the words of Isaiah: "Why spend your money for what is not bread; your wages for what fails to satisfy?" (Is. 55:2).

Yet, even in the West, we know what it is to break through the idle small talk of social gatherings to the real communication of one human soul to another, through the sacred use of the spoken word. This is the kind of dialogue necessary in prayer, for as Isaiah concludes in the same verse, "Heed me, and you shall eat well, you shall delight in rich fare" (Is. 55:2). But for the Western mind, this involves an intentional rethinking of the value of both the human and divine word, as well as a profound renunciation of the superficial for the inner reality of the soul. This is the breakthrough that will take us from the level of social acquaintance to that of lover and dear friend. It is a breakthrough from the idle and profane to the sacred and holy.

This stage corresponds directly to our love relationship with Jesus. At the beginning we are mysteriously affected by the grace of the Holy Spirit so that we are mystically attracted to Jesus. Perhaps we have encountered Him all our life in countless pictures, stories, statues, songs, and sermons. Yet at some point a divine spark ignites the beginnings of a mystical flame of love within our heart. We are attracted to Christ for the first time.

We now want to know more about Jesus. So we read the Bible, look again at sacred paintings or other works of art that reveal the life of Christ. We actually enjoy listening to a preacher or teacher who tells us more about the Jesus we are beginning to love. We start to enjoy the Church again and participate in the sacraments. We may buy and read some spiritual books and hunger for more. This is a strange development for those who have only nominally engaged in these things before. Now we genuinely enjoy them!

In Franciscan prayer this initial stage of dialogue can be called study and meditation. We study and meditate on the objective truths about Jesus as they are revealed in the scriptures and other writings of sacred tradition. Our goal is to discern the voice of Jesus, to learn the desires of His heart. Who is Jesus? What is it He seeks for creation? Who does He desire us to be? Was He gentle, humble, and forgiving? Does He wish us to be the same way? What does He desire for the Church and the world? All these things can be discerned from dialogue with the Lord through spiritual reading, study, and meditation.

In the life of St. Francis we see a similar approach. At a point in his life, Francis became disenchanted with the ways of the secular world. Sparked by grace, he became drawn to solitude, spending days and nights in the shelter of the wooded mountains around Assisi in order to draw close to God. Because of this mystical spark he was drawn to meditate on the crucifix at San Damiano and heard the words of the gospel as a direction for his new life. Contemplating the image of Jesus on a crucifix and hearing the understandable word of Jesus through scriptures, Francis was able to meditate and discern the voice of God as the Word came to him in the initial dialogue of love relationship.

The Understanding of Scripture

This first stage presents to the modern Christian a problem that was not as pronounced in the time of Francis, the understanding of God's voice in scriptures. How do we approach the scriptures when there are now so many different interpretations? Should our approach be literal, as the fundamentalists advocate? Or should all absolutes be written off to cultural influence, as many liberals desire? How can the voice of Jesus in scripture be heard if the scriptures have no singular, credible authority?

To understand these questions, we need first to understand the historical aspect of scriptures. Jesus spoke His words to the apostles and disciples. They, in turn, went forth empowered by the Spirit to "teach all nations" His message (Mt. 28:19). It was because of this personal commission from Jesus Himself that the early Church considered the apostles credible authorities in transmitting His words through preaching and teaching. The apostles, in turn, appointed elders in each Christian community they established, so that their authority would continue to unify the community after they were gone. Later, through the developing life of the Church as it sought to overcome inner conflict and to share the gospel in writing cultures, the words of Jesus were written down by the apostles and their successors. And as the Church continued to grow through questions and conflicts, some of these books were accepted as expressions of the authentic message of Jesus while others were rejected as false. So it can easily be said that the credibility and authority of scripture developed out of the credibility and authority of the early Church. It should be remembered that Jesus promised the gift of the Holy Spirit to the Church, so that Jesus Himself could continue to guide the Church to all truth (Jn. 14:16–18,26; Mt. 28:20).

All this means that the scriptures are to be dynamic, truly able to communicate the living Word of God. They manifest the authority of the God who has poured His living Spirit into a living people, the Church. As such they authoritatively carry forth the words of Jesus who really lived among us. The scriptures are to give life, and are to do so with living authority!

St. Francis encouraged a good, balanced approach to scripture. In the first biographies of his life, we learn how Francis based the brothers' way of life on the literal words of the Gospels. Symbolically, this revelation of his Gospel Rule took place in the bishop's church, directly following the eucharistic liturgy. We read that the brothers' first Rule was composed almost entirely of scriptural quotes and was submitted as such to the pope for approval. This is not unlike St. Paul's experience, who submitted his ministry to the council in Jerusalem for confirmation (Gal. 2: 1-2). It is significant that in Francis's last Testament, dedication to the Church, the priesthood, and the Eucharist precede his reference to the scriptures and the confirmation of his Gospel Rule by the pope. In these examples we see that Francis intuitively sought to balance his approach to scripture with healthy obedience to Church authority and proper eucharistic devotion. Thus he was able to discern and radically live the gospel of Jesus Christ uncompromised, yet within the structure of the Catholic Church.

This is not to belittle the place of scripture in Francis's life. For Francis the word of Jesus was alive. It was not enough to have the legal or intellectual understanding of the written word. The Spirit of Jesus must be understood. In one of his Admonitions Francis says, "a servant of God has been killed by the letter when he has no desire to know the spirit of the Sacred Scripture."

Francis meditated on scripture continually. "Everyday I find such sweetness and consolation in calling to mind and meditating on the humility the Son of God manifested while he was on earth that I could live until the end of the world without hearing or meditating on any other passage from the scriptures." Yet he knew that letter and spirit should only be an aid to the lived experience of a love relationship with Jesus. Thus we read in Bonaventure's life of Francis that for the brothers, "Christ's cross was their book and they studied it day and night." Francis's first biographer, Thomas of Celano, tells of the time Francis gave the brothers' only Bible to a poor woman because he believed "the gift of it will be more pleasing to God than our reading from it."

Francis had a similar approach to theology. He honored theologians and a scholarly study of scripture only when the gospel life of prayer and humility were not destroyed. St. Francis was not "anti-knowledge"; he was against the pride that usually accompanies learning. As he said, "We see many today who would like to attribute honor and glory to themselves by being content with singing about the exploits of others.... Many are they who desire to exalt themselves to the heights of knowledge, but blessed is he who prefers to renounce knowledge for love of the Lord God!" In his letter to St. Anthony, the great preacher and theologian, he gave Anthony permission to teach theology to the friars as long as it did not destroy their prayer. He says quite simply, "It is agreeable to me that you should teach the friars sacred theology, so long as they do not extinguish the spirit of prayer and devotedness over this study, as is contained in the Rule. Farewell."

St. Bonaventure, who became minister general of the Franciscan Order, took a similar avenue in his theological approach to scripture. Throughout the body of his works he consistently held that one cannot begin to understand the scriptures or prayer unless the Holy Spirit enlightened the mind with faith. In his works *The Breviloquium* and *The Collation on the Six Days* he treats the study of scripture at great length. Following the approach of St. Augustine, he did not see the scriptures as a fundamentalistic science textbook where all that is written must be literally true. He did, however, see the essential truth of salvation history authentically transmitted from God through scripture. And he saw the end of scripture leading back to where they must begin: faith in God. The scriptures cannot be understood unless they are studied with faith. Once studied and understood, they strengthen faith. They begin with the Trinity and lead the reader back to the Trinity.

Through all this it can be said there is a place for proper understanding of doctrine, especially at the beginning of our relationship with Jesus. Thus, if we are going to use scripture in our dialogue with Jesus, it is important to understand both their origin and development. Otherwise we might grossly misinterpret Jesus' words to us, greatly hindering the growth of our relationship. This is where the authority of the Church comes in. If there is a passage of scripture that can be interpreted in many opposing ways, we need to go back to the Church from which the scriptures came. When there is substantial agreement on a Church doctrine, then this interpretation should be applied to current situations in a mature way. This will help to ensure the unity of Christ's Body, as well as a balanced, life-giving dynamic in personal scripture meditation.

The Voice of Creation

There is another source beyond the scriptures and sacred writings of the Church we can use in order to hear the Lord's voice. There is all creation, crying out to us to join in her praise of the Creator whom she reveals!

From my own experiences of solitude and silence, I have often found that it is the wonder of nature that teaches me the most profound lessons about God. How many times did the flowing of a creek or the seasonal changes in a tree or flower speak to me during my first hermitage experience? I discovered that nature moves in perfect order, one that defied my limited and human understanding. What we see as order God often sees as limiting, and what we often see as confusion God sees as order. Nature moves in God's order, yet there are few straight lines or perfect squares in the lacework of bare trees against a winter sky! By observing these "pathless paths" we can learn more about the design of the Creator and the eternal ways of God.

Believe it or not, it was from watching the ebb and flow of the creek outside my hermitage door that I learned much about the dynamic and life-giving development of scripture and doctrine within the history of the Church. Three massive trees visible from my hermitage window taught me intuitively, and in the Spirit, of the patience of God and the timeless stability of the Trinity. Through planting, tending, and harvesting my own organic garden, as well as working in an orchard, I learned the values of godly discipline in the alternation between active work and contemplative rest.

Of course, we could all relate similar stories. The flowers that bloom in the Easter season speak to us of the gentle presence of the resurrected Jesus saying "Peace" to His own frightened brothers and sisters. The powerful spring storms with their rushing winds remind us of the giving of the Spirit at Pentecost. There are seemingly countless encounters with nature that reveal the Lord's Word to us in our lifelong dialogue with Him!

I am reminded of a hermitess I know in Wisconsin who lived many years as an active sister in a Catholic teaching order. After years of constant hard work and output she tottered over the line into the proverbial "burnout zone." Tired and confused, she was at least able to discern God's call to make a long retreat in a hermitage.

Ironically, once she reached the hermitage she could not get much out of written material concerning God. She was simply too tired! Only by being still and resting in the gentle arms of "mother nature" did this precious child of God receive the milk of God's Word. As she puts it, "I went into the woods and let the trees minister to me." How many of us have not been in a similar situation in our own lives and have not longed for a similar solution?

Still, some of us tend to be overly skeptical of receiving God's Word through any other means than the scriptures. However, the scriptures themselves immediately impress us with the writers' substantial use of creation imagery to formulate their parables and symbols. The book of the prophet Isaiah relies heavily on nature to communicate the divine message. The psalms are filled with references to the created world that evoke worship and praise in response to the various dimensions of God and His activity among His people.

We know the Lord created the universe, and that after sin entered the world, Jesus reconciled creation to God, "making peace through the blood of his cross" (Col. 1:20). Jesus constantly referred to aspects of nature in His teachings. The birds of the air, the lilies of the field, and the laborers of the fields all spoke to Jesus and were used by Him to communicate divine truths.

Francis, of course, is universally known for his love of creation. His Canticle of the Creatures is the best-known expression of that love. But all his early biographers were quite prolific in describing Francis's affinity with the universe. Thomas of Celano writes, "Hurrying to leave this world inasmuch as it is the place of exile of our pilgrimage, this blessed traveler was yet helped not a little by the things that are in the world. . . . In every work of the artist he praised the Artist; whatever he found in the things made he referred to the Maker. He rejoiced in all the works of the hands of the Lord. . . . In beautiful things he saw Beauty itself; all things were to him good. 'He who made us is best' they cried out to him. Through his footprints impressed upon things he followed the Beloved everywhere; he made for himself from all things a ladder by which to 'come even to his throne'" (Job 23:3).

St. Bonaventure has taken the Poverello's simple love for creation and put it into theological terms pregnant with mystical love. Again insisting that all begins with the gift of faith, Bonaventure consistently says all creation bears the traces of God and will lead the spiritually sensitive observer back to the Trinity through Christ. In other words, if we look and listen with the eyes and ears of faith, all creation will "declare the glory of God" (Ps. 19:1), which is Jesus Christ, the divine Word of the Trinity. Creation can become a prime source of dialogue with Jesus as we seek to grow in our love relationship with Him.

In *The Journey of the Mind to God*, St. Bonaventure's Franciscanism begins to really flower as he says, "The created universe itself is a ladder leading us toward God. Some created things are His traces; others, His image; some of them are material, others spiritual; some temporal, others everlasting: thus some are outside us, and some within." In this he quickly outlines much of his whole work.

Having established that prayer will clear the mind to journey toward God through creation, he goes on to speak of how the cleared mind will perceive God. He simply calls us to look "outside" to find God in the creation, to look "within" to find God within ourselves. This leads us to look "up" to find God in Himself. In all this he returns, again, to the centrality of love relationship with God in his meditation.

Bonaventure says that our use of the creation in meditation involves looking to find God "through" creation and "in" creation. He begins by having us look through the creation when he says, "let us place the first of the ascending rungs at the bottom, by setting before ourselves the whole material world as a mirror through which we can step up to God, the supreme Craftsman." He then goes on to describe how the senses perceive creation to reveal the Creator to our interior selves. He is so convinced that the truly enlightened mind will perceive God through creation that he ends by saying, "Whoever is not enlightened by such brilliance of things created must be blind; whoever is not awakened by their mighty voice must be deaf; whoever fails to praise God for all His works must be dumb; whoever fails to discover the First Principle through all these signs must be a fool.

"Open your eyes, then, alert your spiritual ears, unseal your lips and apply your heart, so that in all creatures you may see, hear, praise, love and serve, glorify and honor your God, lest the whole world rise against you."

Here Bonaventure's Franciscan charism is shining brightly. As Francis wrote the Canticle of the Creatures in praise of God, so Bonaventure now writes with the same spirit as he sees all of creation leading the pure mind back to the Creator through meditation. But this is not some passionless, cool ascent. It is the ascent prompted by a passionate love for Christ, which prompts even Bonaventure to join with Francis in a spontaneous outburst of praise!

Bonaventure begins the second chapter by moving from seeing God "through" creation to seeing God "in" creation. He says, "Taking perceptible things as a mirror, we see God through them—through His traces, so to speak; but we also see Him in them, as He is there by His essence, power and presence. This view is loftier than the first. Thus, it holds the next higher place, as the second rung of contemplation, where we are led to contemplate God in all the creatures that enter our mind through the bodily senses."

It would be good to note here that he is not advocating some form of pantheism, where God is a tree, flower, or some other aspect of nature. Bonaventure always maintains God's transcendence as being beyond the created world in His fullness and self-sufficiency, yet in His goodness, emanating by choice into the creation. Thus, Bonaventure accomplishes the same unity between God and creation attempted by pantheism. By seeing God as emanating into creation, rather than being creation, he does not lose sight of God's "otherliness" or transcendence. This balanced approach is much more in keeping with the full human experience of all creation and our personal yet transcendent God. Bonaventure greatly respects God's transcendence in his complete understanding of mystical prayer especially as he moves into the concept of divine darkness which comes from the Christian East.

In chapter three Bonaventure moves from contemplating God "through" and "in" His "traces" in creation to contemplating God as His "image" is reflected in the mirror of the human self. As he says, "The two preceding steps, by drawing us to God through His traces as reflected in all creatures, have led us to a point where we enter into our own self, that is, our own mind, in which is reflected His very Image. Therefore, at this third stage, by entering our own self, as if leaving the outer court, we must endeavor to see God through this mirror in the 'Holy Place' (Ex. 28:34) or forward section of the 'Dwelling.' As the 'Lampstand' there sheds light, even so, the light of truth is ever glowing on the face of our mind; which is to say that the image of the most blessed Trinity very brightly shines upon it . . . . Go into yourself, therefore."

It is clear that Bonaventure's writings give much support to our modern emphasis on self-awareness. However, he avoids the danger of self-centeredness by teaching the classical Christian position on humility. Humility is just the truth about ourselves. True self-awareness must by its very nature lead us to humility before our Creator, rather than to the pride that separates us from Him, His creation, and even ourselves. But contemplated rightly, the human self that finds its true value in being created in God's image will lead us back to contemplation of God.

Sin and Grace

Why is it so many people who advocate self-awareness do not advocate the existence of God? Bonaventure deals directly with this question in the later chapters of *The Journey of the Mind to God* saying, "In view of the clear truth of God's extreme closeness to our mind, it might seem extraordinary that so few people should be aware of the First Principle within themselves. Yet the reason is obvious: the human mind, distracted by worldly cares, fails to enter into itself through Memory; clouded by imagination, it fails to turn toward itself through Intelligence; attracted by concupiscence, it fails to return to itself through Desire for inner sweetness and spiritual joy. Immersed in the sense, it is unable to re-enter into itself as into the likeness of God." He clearly understands that sin is not so much the direct opposition of a person to God's truth, but a person getting sidetracked on the way to God. It is the slight perversion of a truth that, in time, leads to great error.

The word "sin" was originally used in archery tournaments when an arrow missed the bull's-eye. Notice that the arrow could have hit anywhere else on the target, but to miss the bull's-eye was called a "sin." It missed the perfection of being totally centered. By this definition we are all sinners. We all come very close to pefection in a few areas of our spiritual life, but even our best falls short of absolute perfection. We might even do very well in every area of our life, considering ourselves to be "well-rounded" men and women. But we still miss that perfection of total centeredness in God when left to our unaided human effort.

It is like a ship that sets sail across a vast ocean but has set its bearings one degree off its desired course. At first, the mistake in navigation is hardly noticeable. But after many days at sea it becomes evident that the ship is headed into the wrong region. Finally, the ship will reach shore, only to find it is miles and miles from its original, hoped-for destination.

Sin is the same way. We head off in a generally right direction, but are somehow still off-center, maybe only by an almost imperceptible amount. But after a longer period of time, these areas become noticeably destructive in our life and in the lives of those we know and love. At first we seem only to enjoy the things of the earth with a spirit of "take it or leave it." But soon it becomes clear we are in bondage to materialism and lust. For instance, we eat only a little too much, but soon we have stolen from the hungry and entered blatantly into the sin of gluttony. This pattern, of course, applies to all areas of our life. What began as a tiny misuse of a good thing, becomes after habitual misuse a dark and destructive force in our life with God and humankind.

This is what Bonaventure is speaking of in the above quote, and why he will insist that human effort in religion without the grace of God's inspiration and revelation will lead nowhere. He says, "we cannot rise above ourselves unless a superior power lifts us up. No matter how well we plan our spiritual progress, nothing comes of it unless divine assistance intervenes. And divine assistance is there for those who seek it humbly and devoutly . . . by fervent prayer. Prayer, then, is the mother and the beginning of the ascent." Bonaventure then maintains the Pauline theme of man's inability to find enlightenment without God's grace saying, "If a man falls into a pit, he will lie there until someone reaches down to help him out." In the same way, it was impossible for man to rise completely from the pit of the senses to the true seeing of themselves, and, within themselves, of Eternal Truth, until that Truth, assuming human nature in the Person of Christ, became unto them a ladder, restoring the first ladder broken by Adam.

"Enlightened though a man may be by natural and acquired knowledge, he cannot enter into himself there to take delight in the Lord (Ps. 36:4), except through Christ."

Here he sees the light of Jesus Christ as the power that will dispel our darkness and heal us of our blindness. As Bonaventure says, we cannot properly reflect the image of God if the mirror of our mind is not first cleansed of sin and polished through love. But once we are cleansed of the sins that dull the image of God within us, and blind us to the image of God without, then our soul can journey to God through contemplating the creation with eyes opened by divine grace.

Human Being and God's Oneness

When the eyes of our spiritual perception have been cleansed by grace, then we perceive God by looking into creation for His traces and into the human self for His image. The very fact of our being human reflects the being of God. The fact that each healthy human soul is multifaceted yet united as one being implies that God is diverse, yet one Being. This is foundational in all monotheistic religions (Mk. 12:29; Ex. 20:3).

But the existence of God is not seen as a static concept of dry theology for the Franciscan. Contemplation of God's being and God's oneness elevates the perceptive soul into the heights of mystical paradox and divine wonder. God is alive! God is infinite! God's oneness is so infinite that it appears to bring together conflicting extremes in a paradoxical coincidence of opposites. God is at once perceived by the grace-filled soul, and still beyond the grasp of the limited mind.

Bonaventure establishes the awesome reality of God's being and the mystical paradoxes of its dimensions by saying, "Because the utterly pure and the most absolute being . . . is the very first and last, it is the origin and final end of all things. Because it is eternal and all present, surrounding and penetrating all duration, it is, as it were, both their center and their circumference. Because it is utterly simple and utterly great, it is wholly interior to all things and wholly exterior to them. 'It is an intelligible sphere, the center of which is everywhere, and the circumference nowhere.' Because it is supremely actual and immutable, 'while remaining unmoved, it imparts motion to all.' Because it is wholly perfect and wholly immeasurable, it is interior to all things, yet not enclosed; exterior to all things, yet not excluded; above all things, yet not aloof; below all things, yet not their servant. For, truly, it is supremely one and all inclusive: therefore, even though all things are many and pure being is but one, it is all in all." So it is that the Seraphic Doctor moves beyond the mundane of mere intellectual speculation in his theology and breaks through to the mystical and divine.

The Trinity and the Human Soul

For many modern Christians, the Trinity is not so much a mystical reality as a passively accepted doctrine. We accept Jesus with our heart, but we accept the Trinity with our mind. In the Christian East this is not the case. The contemplatives of the East will speak of the indwelling Trinity as the mystical goal of their meditation and contemplation. From experiencing the mystery of the Trinity within their souls, they come to understand unity in the midst of an often complex and seemingly disjointed human existence. This brings rest and peace. However, in the West the Trinity has been reduced to a doctrine to be studied by seminary students, rarely the object of our own personal prayer.

I have found the deep trinitarian mysticism of Bonaventure to be extremely relevant for me in today's Christian world. Though centuries removed from all our "high tech" insight into personality, his simple understanding of the human soul and its ability to reflect its Creator has renewed in me an understanding and awareness of my beloved triune God. It has also increased in me an appreciation for the purpose of true self-awareness, so often used as an excuse for a "do your own thing" (or in this case, "believe your own thing") mentality.

True self-awareness, according to Bonaventure, will lead us almost by instinct back to faith in a triune God, quite different from the popular and perhaps comfortable though vaguely agnostic concept of the "One God" of a single entity. Still, many honest seekers are confused by the possibility of a triune God for the very good reason that it sounds suspiciously like "three gods in one," which is hardly the revelation of God who said, "Hear, O Israel, the Lord your God is One!" Nor was it Bonaventure's goal to complicate the issue further by dividing the main functions of the soul into its own trinity: memory, intellect, will. Actually, his theory simplifies matters by showing in just what manner man was made and thereby reflects the image of his Creator. Through memory, we are led to contemplate the eternal nature of God; through intellect we discover the absolute, universal truth of God; and our will teaches us the possibility of an infinitely loving God.

Granted, the soul's reflection of an eternal, true, and loving God does not necessarily indicate a trinity of Persons in that Godhead. However, it was not Bonaventure's purpose (nor should it be ours) to defend the Christian revelation so much as it was to show the genius and simple beauty present in the creation's capacity to be "the visible sign of invisible light." For, in Bonaventure's thinking, our memory begets knowledge in the intellect, and these two together bring forth the "breath of love," which joins the two and shows itself in the acts of the will. Thus, "these three—the begetting mind, the word, and love—exist in the soul, paralleling memory, intelligence, and will, which are consubstantial, coequal and coeval, and also interacting." So, when we contemplate these functions of the human soul, we rise as if through a mirror, "to the vision of the Holy Trinity, Father, Word and Love: who are co-eternal, coeval and consubstantial, so that each exists in the others, but none is either of the others, although the three are one God."

Meditation on our desire and capacity for goodness, Bonaventure says, will also lead us to know and believe that God is triune. For goodness, to be full and complete, must be selfless and self-diffusive. But how can it be unless God is both one in being and plural in persons within Himself? With whom, then, could He share His own goodness before the creation of the universe? This does not mean that goodness necessitated God's creation of the universe, according to the "God is lonely" theory. If God were limited by loneliness and looking to complete Himself in another, that goodness would make God dependent on the created world, destroying both His transcendence and self-sufficiency.

But the Trinity is fulfilled within itself, by the eternal begottenness of the Son from the Father, and the eternal spiration of the Spirit from the love union of the Father and Son. The Father is the fountain of fullness, whose goodness overflows without and through eternity to both Son and Spirit. Thus, eternally fulfilled with the triune oneness, God is free to create the universe from that goodness by choice rather than by necessity. And we are free to adore! Indeed, adoration is the only possible response left us, for we will never fully understand the mystery of the holy Trinity. Even Bonaventure recognized his limitations on this score and warns us, "But while studying these matters, beware of thinking that you comprehend the incomprehensible; for there are other things to be considered. . . ." Still, as Bonaventure says, "Who would not be lifted up in wonder on beholding such marvels?"

Yes, true self-awareness can lead us to a very deep awareness of God. The very consciousness of our existence will bring us into the presence of the God who calls Himself

"I Am," for in His being "we move and breathe and have our being" (Acts 17:28). Yet within this simple perception we will be led even further to contemplate the mystical wonders of God as Trinity, the source of our own trinitarian character. There, in our eternally good God, we will find our own capacity for goodness, whose goodness flows selflessly from Person to Person in perfect Trinity for all eternity without losing the divine oneness of His being, or the goodness He freely gives to creation in space and time. Finally, since nobody can fully understand the depths of a person except the spirit of that person (1 Cor. 2:11), the mystery of our own human soul will lead us to stand in awe and wonder before the infinite mystery of our trinitarian yet one God. So, as St. Francis encourages, "let us always make in us a tabernacle and dwelling place for Him who is the Lord God omnipotent, Father, Son and Holy Ghost," and the divine Trinity will cease to be abstract, unapproachable—a theological concept; He will be the Trinity accepted by the heart, as close and relevant to us as the existence of our own human soul.

The Incarnation

As we learn to find God in oneness and Trinity by contemplating our human soul, we also come to contemplate Jesus, the complete incarnation of divinity in humanity. True, we are all human and divine in that we have been created in the image of God and restored to that image through the grace of God in Christ. This was clearly understood by St. Francis, who wrote in his Admonitions, "Try to realize the dignity God has conferred on you. He created and formed your body in the image of his beloved Son, and your soul in his own likeness." Indeed, "God created man in his image; in the divine image he created him; male and female he created them" (Gen. 1:27). Yet

Francis took it a step further in recognizing that man is fallen and therefore no longer reflects his Creator except as in a cracked mirror. "And yet every creature under heaven serves and acknowledges and obeys its Creator in its own way better than you do. Even the devils were not solely responsible for crucifying him; it was you who crucified him with them and you continue to crucify him by taking pleasure in your vices and sins."

Where then can we look for a vision of the perfection we have lost? Obviously, the answer lies in Him in whom all the fullness of God was pleased to dwell (Col. 1:19), Jesus Christ, Son of God and Son of Mary. What occurs in part within us occurs completely in "The glorious Word of the Father . . . made known to the glorious and blessed Virgin Mary, in whose womb he took on our weak human nature." With these opening words in his "Letter to All the Faithful," Francis exalts in the mystery of the incarnation on which he meditated daily, and we are challenged to imitate this man who "would recall Christ's words through persistent meditation and bring to mind his deeds through the most penetrating consideration." Francis believed the incarnation to be one of the two greatest deeds accomplished by Christ, the other being His passion.

Thus, what we see partially within ourselves, our brothers, and our sisters, we see completely when we turn our eyes to Christ. But let us not shun contemplation of our human soul, for Bonaventure assures us that "this consideration brings about perfect enlightening of the mind, when the mind beholds man made, as on the sixth day, in the image of God." So when we contemplate in Christ the Son of God "our own humanity so wonderfully exalted and so ineffably present in Him, and when we thus behold in one and the same Being both the first and the last, the highest and the lowest, the circumference and the center, the Alpha and the Omega, the caused and the cause, the Creator and the creature ... then our mind at last reaches a perfect object.... Nothing more is to come but the day of quiet, on which, in an ecstatic intuition, the human mind rests after all its labors." This intuition will teach us to see His completeness even while gazing upon a humankind that is yet incomplete. What a great and wonderful mystery, that by gazing upon the human soul, we are led to contemplate the divine mystery of Christ's incarnation; by considering the incarnation we find ourselves "hidden now with Christ in God" (Col. 3:3).

Visualization

Dialoguing with Jesus through His traces in creation, His image in people, and His words in scripture implies a move beyond perception of externals to the interior dimension of meditation. Remember Francis's emphasis on moving past the intellectual realities in order to apprehend the spirit of sacred writings. In life and words, he stressed that study must not hinder prayer but serve it. The scriptures encourage us also to "meditate on the law of the Lord day and night" (Ps. 1:2). In his letter to the Romans, St. Paul urges: "Be transformed by the renewal of your mind." In the book of Proverbs we are told: "As a man thinketh in his heart, so is he." These and many more scriptural passages encourage us to meditate on all the various ways God speaks to us of His will. So we are led back into relationship with Him through meditation.

In all this the process of visualization is very important. As psychologists have pointed out, we think in symbols and images, not in abstract concepts. Even when we think of things like mathematical formulas, we still see pictures of the numbers in our minds.

In Franciscan meditation the practice of visualizing the life of Jesus has been very important. Francis, "a poet whose whole life was a poem," loved to teach by symbolic action rather than by word. One example is his reenactment of the Christmas story at the little town of Greccio. Thomas of Celano describes the historic event, noting that the birth of this now world-celebrated tradition was simply the natural overflow of Francis's constant preoccupation with the "humility of the incarnation" which "occupied his memory . . . to the extent he wanted to think of hardly anything else." Thus, Francis fathered the first reenactment of the manger scene at Bethlehem. "I wish to do something that will recall to memory the little Child who was born in Bethlehem and set before our bodily eyes in some way the inconveniences of his infant needs, how he lay in a manger, how, with an ox and an ass standing by, he lay upon the hay where he had been placed. . . . The day of joy drew near, the time of great rejoicing came. The brothers were called from their various places. Men and women of that neighborhood prepared with glad hearts candles and torches to light up that night that has lighted up all the days and years with its gleaming star. . . . The manger was prepared. . . . There simplicity was honored, poverty was exalted, humility was commended, and Greccio was made, as it were, a new Bethlehem."

And then there was the time when the Poverello was asked to preach a sermon to St. Clare and her sisters. "When the nuns had come together . . . Francis raised his eyes to heaven, where his heart always was, and began to pray to Christ. He commanded ashes to be brought to him and he made a circle with them around himself . . . and sprinkled the rest of them on his head. . . . The blessed father remained standing in the circle in silence. . . . The saint then suddenly rose and to the amazement of the nuns recited the 'Miserere mei Deus' in place of a sermon. . . . By his actions he taught them that they should regard themselves as ashes."

How many times Francis taught by actions, burning into the mind of the beholder a vivid image and symbol of Christlikeness!

St. Bonaventure was much influenced by the primitive expressiveness of Francis. In *The Mystical Vine* and *The Tree of Life*, Bonaventure encourages meditation on the life of Jesus by visualizing the crucifixion in graphic detail. He writes of meditation through spiritual reading in *The Triple Way*, and on God's traces and images in creation in *The Mind's Journey to God*. In all these works, internalization of outer perceptions by means of visualization is central. As he says in the prologue of *The Tree of Life*, "Contemplate with vivid representation, penetrating intelligence, and loving will—the labors, the suffering, and the love of Jesus crucified, so that he can repeat with the Bride: 'A bundle of myrrh is my Beloved to me; He shall abide between my breasts.'"

"Imagination assists understanding," says Bonaventure. And he encourages the reader of *The Tree of Life* to "picture in your imagination." He then goes on to develop a detailed visualization of the Tree of Life which symbolizes the life of Jesus and His Church in vivid images. From the above quote it is easy to perceive how St. Bonaventure saw a personal love relationship with Jesus as the Beloved as being the end purpose of all Christian meditation. Whether contemplating the word of Jesus coming to us through creation, the self, or the scriptures, Bonaventure always ends his meditation with a rapturous proclamation of the mystical beauty of this love relationship between the Lover and the Beloved.

Of course the development of devotional practices and art in Franciscan tradition demonstrates what priority visualized meditation had in the mystical life. One such example is the Way of the Cross, developed by Leonard of Port Maurice (1676–1751) at the hermitage of Fonte Columbo.

This visual meditation is a way of entering into and understanding the passion of Jesus without ponderous theological study. In praying the Franciscan crown rosary, given by revelation to a young friar of the fifteenth century, we imaginatively share with Mary the joyful and glorious mysteries of Jesus. Simple and quiet meditation on these truths is often more life-changing than any amount of study. Francis's loving creation of the Christmas crib, now a world-wide tradition, depicts the birth of Jesus for us more eloquently than a theological treatise on the incarnation. But would we have this tradition if Francis had not taken the time to fix the picture of the Infant in his heart?

Later in history the Friars initiated the use of mystery plays, designed to reach the average man with the life and gospel of Christ. Performed in the street, these festive theaters would often begin in one locale, winding their way eventually to the Friars' churches. Franciscan churches have always been known for the simple directness of their decor. Stepping in from the hot sun to the cool interior, a man could see again in statues, windows, and paintings the story just acted for his benefit. All art was an attempt to join with Francis in allowing the symbol to penetrate the mind more deeply and lastingly than words.

In today's culture we might find many of these practices a clutter of images that actually hinder meditation. Yet, for the cultures in which they grew, these devotions were created to facilitate authentic Christian meditation through visualization. Today, because we are a reading culture, many of these practices are not as relevant as they once were. Yet, even today, we would be intellectually conceited to think we have moved beyond the need for symbols and some "visual aids" for meditation within our places of worship.

Summary

This all means beginning our prayer by being open to the mystery of Christ, who is seen incarnated in the created world, yet still remains the transcendent Creator. It is not enough simply to read the scriptures. We must visualize the events we are reading and enter into those accounts through the creative use of imagination and visualization. Nor is it enough to give nature merely a "passing glance." We must immerse ourselves in the sounds, smells, and sensations of nature and wait for the Lord to speak through the world He created. Yet this cannot happen unless we open our imagination in a healthy, creative way while we sojourn in the woods, the garden, or the desert. Finally, it is never enough to take human beings at face value. As a good friend of mine once said, "I am an icon of God"—much more important than wood or stone. If we look beneath the human dimension creatively and positively, we will discover in this veil of flesh a reflection of the divine. Even Jesus Himself looked like a typical human being at first glance; so will these other areas reveal only the natural and the obvious at first. However, with a more creative look through a healthy use of visualization and imagination, the scriptures, creation, and the human soul will begin to manifest the real and living Word, who is the incarnation of God Himself.

I set aside a time every morning for such meditations or visualizations with scripture. Between my rising at 5:30 a.m. and my community prayer at 7:30 a.m., I sit very quietly in my hermitage and ponder a passage or two from the Bible. This allows me time to let just a few words soak in like a gentle spring rain or a soft winter snow.

I begin by visualizing in my mind very clearly who is speaking—Jesus, Paul, or one of the prophets—and imagine the circumstances surrounding the particular event. I set them in a typical, Middle Eastern countryside or in the Holy Land where they lived. Soon the smells and sounds of a primitive Middle Eastern village stir in my mind, the desert sand is hot beneath my feet, and the woolen tunic feels rough around my own body. As this scene comes to life, I then let the words speak to me. From this "real-life" setting I find it easier to translate those words into my daily walk with the Lord.

Speaking of walks, I have found long walks in the woods around my hermitage to be a great aid in my prayer. Here I put aside all my responsibilities and worries of community life or ministry. I just walk and, much as the Lord walked in the Garden of Eden in the cool of the evening, I truly expect Jesus to walk with me. I breathe the fresh mountain air, notice the moisture clinging to a twig, or watch the tiniest creatures about their daily chores. In all these things I let myself "feel" the life of the forest. I must "experience" and "know" the forest, for in so doing I become one with my divine Lover, who created all things.

During those walks I will often visualize Jesus or a great saint walking close by. I see Jesus transfigured when I reach the tops of our small Ozark mountains. I see St. Francis with me when I wander for an afternoon or pray within one of our many caves. All this brings me very close to the reality of their presence with and around me every moment of my life.

I have also learned to find God in people. I look for His eyes in their gaze and listen for His words in their speaking. I have learned to find His love in their love.

Within myself, as well, I have found God. I marvel that when I long for love, I reflect that my Creator, my God, is love. Searching for truth, I reflect that God is the final and absolute truth. Conscious of the movement of time, I reflect God's eternal nature. All my human characteristics reflect a counterpart in the divine nature of God and find their fulfillment in Him. I always try to praise my Creator when meditating on these reflections of God that exist within my own soul.

Surrounded by such loveliness—loveliness within and loveliness without—how can I then help but repeat St. Teresa of Avila's own cry: "O Beauty containing all beauty; thou art strength itself, thou art truth, Lord, and the genuine riches: do thou reign forever."

I strongly encourage everyone to make his or her whole life an opportunity for such prayer and visualization. Set aside time to meditate on the scriptures for a few minutes every day. Take walks in the park or go to the rural areas regularly. See all those around you—your family, friends, those with whom you work—as opportunities to see God reflected there, for are we not all "gazing on the Lord's glory with unveiled faces, being transformed from glory to glory into his very image" (2 Cor. 3:18)? Finally, learn to see your own longings and desires as the mirrors of God's nature, who will fulfill and perfect all that concerns you, for God will "supply your needs fully, in a way worthy of His magnificent riches in Christ Jesus" (Phil. 4:19).

In this way all the world will become an occasion to walk and dialogue with Jesus. You will hear Him in the silence and in the noise. You will find Him in the solitude of the wilderness or in the close-quartered city. You will always be with Him even when you are totally by yourself, or alone with Him even when you are with others. Learn to visualize Him with you at all times, and you will be able to dialogue with Jesus throughout your whole day until the end of your life. You will draw very close to your divine Lover and discover in your own experience that of Francis's, whose "daily and continuous talk was of Jesus and how sweet and tender his conversation was, how kind and filled with love was his talk. His mouth 'spoke out of the abundance of his heart,' and the fountain of enlight-

ened love that filled his whole being bubbled forth out-
wardly. Indeed, he was always occupied with Jesus; Jesus
he bore in his heart, Jesus in his mouth, Jesus in his ears,
Jesus in his eyes, Jesus in his hands, Jesus in the rest of his
members. O how often, when he sat down to eat, hearing
or speaking or thinking of Jesus, he forgot bodily food. . . .
Indeed, as he went along the way meditating on and singing of Jesus, he would forget his journey and invite all the
elements to praise Jesus."

3
LOVE UNION

⚜

The next stage of communication between the Lover
and the Beloved moves beyond words and thoughts into
the pure love touch of mystical union. Divine body begins
to touch human body and divine heart beats against
human heart until they become one through the existen-
tial outpouring of the Holy Spirit. The culmination of this
nonverbal communication is the total union of spiritual
intercourse. Lover and Beloved die to themselves and
become one. As a result, new life is created as the children
of the Church are brought forth from this love union.

As we have already said, following St. Paul's lead in
Ephesians 5:32, we can learn much from the relationship
between a husband and wife that applies to our relationship with Jesus as His Bride. In fact, Jesus' own words call
us to "know" Him (Mt. 7:23) as a man knows his wife in
sexual intercourse (Gen. 4:1). This tells us a great deal
about the spiritual sexuality and passion involved in a truly
intimate mystical union with Christ.

However, this analogy can be upsetting to those who
are not culturally used to speaking in such language about
our relationship with Jesus. It might be considered irrever-
ent, distasteful, or embarrassing. It is especially difficult for
the man who feels he must live up to the American "macho"

image to consider himself Jesus' Bride. To think of Jesus as Lord or brother is quite acceptable; to think of Him as Husband or Lover calls for an abandonment that makes many squirm in their seats.

It is interesting to note Francis's approach to this spiritual sexuality. He has no trouble with the female dimension of his relationship with Jesus. In the "Letter to All the Faithful" he writes: "A person is His Bride when his faithful soul is united with Jesus Christ by the Holy Spirit." Not only this but, "we are mothers to Him when we enthrone Him in our hearts and souls by love with a pure and sincere conscience and give birth to Him by doing good." Francis frequently likened the relationship of a minister in leadership to his brothers to that between a mother and her sons. These examples show that Francis recognized the *anima* and *animus*, or male and female qualities within us all. We are encouraged, as his brothers were by him, to develop some of the more feminine qualities of tenderness and gentleness in our relationship with God and one another.

Many different dimensions to this love relationship between the Lover and the Beloved are brought out by a fuller understanding of familiar scriptures. If we look at these scriptures in light of this analogy—the Church as Bride, and Jesus as Groom—many new mystical insights and subtleties come to us. For instance, we know that in the first letter to the Corinthians Paul describes the Church as the Body of Christ, and that he uses this analogy in many of his letters. But why? Is it only because we are filled, or impregnated, with the Spirit of Christ that we are called the body of Christ as well? Another text is the much disputed Pauline teaching on the mutual submission between husband and wife in Ephesians 5:21–33. In this case, many modern cultural problems need to be overcome before perceiving the timeless mystical truth surrounding the role of the spiritual Bride and the divine Groom.

In this scripture the "Body of Christ" becomes synonymous with the "Bride of Christ," even as the body of a bride becomes an extension and possession of the body of her husband. Paul's whole reason for writing this is to prompt the husband to a more Christlike love and concern for his wife. Nonetheless, from this analogy Paul reveals a mystical secret to show how the spiritual Bride becomes the extension and possession of the actual Body of Christ, and so is properly called by that name. This whole analogy is further punctuated and clarified by 1 Corinthians 7:4, where St. Paul writes, "The woman has no rights over her own body; it is the husband who has them. In the same way, the husband has no rights over his body; the wife has them."

We can see that the Church is called the "Body of Christ" because she is, in fact, the "Bride of Christ." As such, our "body" becomes the Lord's Body as He takes possession of our whole life. As St. Paul says in Galatians 2:20, "The life I live now is not my own, but Christ is living in me."

Galatians 5:22–25 sheds even more light on how Jesus "takes possession" of the Bride. In it, Paul exhorts the Church, the Body and Bride of Christ, to bear the fruit of the Spirit. What is a fruit? Isn't a fruit an impregnated womb in the reproduction process of a plant? Think of it: A flower blossom on a fruit tree is fertilized and grows into a seed-bearing fruit. The fruit slowly ripens until it falls off the tree. As it rots, the fruit protects the seed and fertilizes the soil. Hopefully, the seed will lodge in the fertile soil to sprout someday into a new fruit tree. Then the process will begin again.

So, to extend the metaphor, St. Paul calls the Bride of Christ to become impregnated by the Spirit. This implies a spiritual version of sexual intercourse that causes the Bride to manifest the spiritual pregnancy in her life by the "fruit of the Spirit." When the pregnancy of the Spirit is complete, our lives will be radically transformed by this fruit, and we will bring forth new children in Christ (Gal. 4:19), those we meet and know who come to be "born again" of the Spirit (Jn. 3: 3–5) through the witness of our life (Acts 1:8).

St. Paul speaks of those he has brought into faith in Christ as his children. In one letter he speaks to the local church as a mother to a disobedient child. "You are my children, and you put me back in labor pains until Christ is formed in you" (Gal. 4:19). It is interesting to note that Paul also puts himself in the role of a father helping to birth spiritual children (1 Cor. 4:14–15; 2 Cor. 6:13). So, even with his ability to speak as a father to his spiritual children, Paul can also speak as a mother to a nursing child. "On the contrary, when we were among you we were gentle as any nursing mother fondling her little ones" (1 Thess. 2:7). This is why he could write to the spiritual infants at Corinth and say he spoke to them "as infants in Christ: I fed you with milk, and did not give you solid food because you were not ready for it" (1 Cor. 3:1–2).

What I write here is nothing new. This whole metaphor is described graphically in St. Bonaventure's "On the Five Feasts of the Child Jesus." In this work he says, "When this devout soul . . . receives the visit of new inspiration, becomes inflamed with holy desire, and feels the pressure of heavenly thought . . . it is made spiritually fruitful by the spirit of grace . . . what is all this if not the act of the Father making the soul pregnant?" He even goes on to speak of a "morning sickness" which is likened to our turning from the things of the world! "After this most holy conception, the soul assumes a pale countenance. . . . Food and drink cease to appeal to the mind because of complete contempt and rejection of worldly things. . . . Sometimes the soul even begins to weaken and languish because of mortification of self-will. . . . All external, visible things of the world begin to seem tedious and burdensome, as offending the One perceived and sensed within the soul."

It is significant that Bonaventure calls us to be a spiritual Mary in this whole process. After impregnation "the soul groans as it begins its journey with Mary into the hill country," and giving birth to Jesus must be full of this identification. "Remember first that you must be Mary. . . . From such a Mary, Jesus Christ does not disdain to be spiritually born." Calling us to present the Child to the Father in profound worship he says, "Go up, therefore, O spiritual Mary, no longer into the hill country, but into the dwelling place of the spiritual Jerusalem, into the palace of the heavenly city. And there, before the throne of the eternal Trinity and undivided Unity, humbly kneel in spirit; present your Son to God the Father, praising, blessing, and glorifying the Father, the Son, and the Holy Spirit."

At the beginning of this work Bonaventure speaks of his own experience of being impregnated by the Spirit. "As I had occasion to withdraw for a while from the turmoil of distracting thoughts, and to enter into my inner self in silent meditation, I came to wonder which aspect of the divine Incarnation I should consider, in order to obtain spiritual consolation. . . . In the secret of my mind, I saw that, with the grace of the Holy Spirit, a soul devoted to God could conceive the blessed Word, the only-begotten Son of God the Father; that it could give birth to Him. . . ." Here Bonaventure alludes to the discipline of silence, solitude, and controlled meditation needed to serve as the proper environment or setting for the love union to take place between the Beloved and her divine Lover.

Sexual intercourse is a special gift shared between a husband and a wife. It is a sacramental symbol that helps to increase their love, when experienced in a sensitive and meaningful way. Time and place must be set aside so that no interruptions disturb the natural flow of the love exchange. Time is often taken for sensitive conversation at the beginning of the experience. Then, almost without noticing, communication becomes nonverbal as the husband and wife begin to embrace and kiss with tender touches of love. After this foreplay, the woman will open to the man, and the man will enter the woman. At this point the woman totally abandons her body to the man while the man freely gives his body to the woman. This moment of death is also a moment of bliss. It is the ultimate emotional high, yet it is totally for the sake of the other. It is from this mutual death in giving oneself for the other that life is born.

The same holds true in the mystical love union between Jesus and His Bride. This, too, is a special gift for which we must set aside special times and places to become one with our Lover through prayer. As with a husband and wife, prayer usually begins with dialogue or visualized meditation. Then we move almost unnoticeably into a nonconceptual communion that is experienced in pure and tender "love touches" between Lover and Beloved. Soon we open totally to Jesus in total trust and abandon. He enters our very body and impregnates us with His Holy Spirit in a spiritual climax that is both our ultimate emotional fulfillment of self and our most complete abandonment of and death to self. We give our body and life to Jesus, and He gives His body and life for His Bride through His passion, death, and resurrection. Further, He has given each of us His Spirit in our own personal Pentecost. From this union we grow full of new life, pregnant with the life-changing fruit of the Spirit. Then, when we grow to spiritual maturity, like St. Paul we give birth to new spiritual children within the Church.

St. John of the Cross speaks of the mystical union, or "love touch," of this spiritual sexuality when he says in his beautiful poetry:

Upon my flowering breast
which I kept wholly for Him alone,
there He lay sleeping
and I caressing Him
there in a breeze from the fanning cedars.
When the breeze blew from the turret
parting His hair,
He wounded my neck
with His gentle hand,
suspending all my senses.

Or again,

Bride:

In the inner wine cellar
I drank of my Beloved.
There He gave me His breast;
there He taught me a sweet
*   and living knowledge*
and I gave myself to Him,
keeping nothing back;
there I promised to be His Bride.

Bridegroom:

The Bride has entered
the sweet garden of her desire,
and she rests in delight,
laying her neck
on the gentle arms of her Beloved.
Beneath the apple tree:
There I took you for My own,
there I offered you My hand,
and I restored you,
where your mother was corrupted.

These lines of poetry are applied by John to various
stages of the mystical life, but they do indicate the graphic

language John uses to describe the love touch of mystical union between the Lover and the Beloved. Furthermore, by reading John of the Cross's commentaries on his mystical poems, we can clearly perceive that he, too, emphasized the necessity of passing through the stage of "dialogue" before we enter into the stage of pure "love touch."

In Franciscan mysticism this stage of "love touch" is often spoken of as rapture. In rapture, one is touched by God so completely, or consummately, that one is "caught up" totally out of oneself. It is a union so deeply involving the emotions and the body that it totally overwhelms the person, who is often deemed as being in a "trance" or "slain in the Spirit."

The Experience of Rapture

In his little book entitled *Franciscan Mysticism*, Brother Boniface Maes says about this rapture: "The grace of God sometimes overflows like a river and invades the emotional powers of the soul . . . there follows spiritual intoxication, which is a breaking out of overwhelming tenderness and delicious intimacies greater than the heart can desire or contain."

We are reminded here of the "intoxication" of the Spirit experienced by the first Christians at Pentecost. "When the day of Pentecost came it found them gathered in one place. Suddenly from up in the sky there came a noise like a strong, driving wind which was heard all through the house where they were seated. Tongues as of fire appeared, which parted and came to rest on each of them. All were filled with the Holy Spirit. They began to express themselves in foreign tongues and make bold proclamations as the Spirit prompted them." As Peter had to go on to explain to those who heard them speaking, "You must realize that these men are not drunk, as you seem to think. It is only nine in the morning" (Acts 2:1–4). He then goes on to quote the prophet Joel to explain that they are intoxicated by the Spirit which has been "poured out" upon them. St. Paul alludes to the same intoxication when he says, "Avoid getting drunk on wine; that leads to debauchery. Be filled with the Spirit, addressing one another in psalms and hymns and inspired songs. Sing praise to the Lord with all your hearts" (Eph. 5:18–19).

How many times has this been true in my life! Touched by the flame of the Spirit, my heart fills with joy to the point that I feel it must explode in an outburst of praise. Yet, what words exist that adequately describe the experience of the Spirit so far beyond words? As T. S. Eliot so eloquently says,

> . . . *Words strain,*
> *Crack and sometimes break, under the burden,*
> *Under the tension, slip, slide, perish,*
> *Decay with imprecision* . . .

But united to God, I burst forth into new songs, melodies without words, or words I have never heard before. At other times I break down and cry tears of boundless joy. Many times I am left dumbfounded by an awesome silence into which words can barely reach, and music imitates only from a distance. It is here that I learn what a thousand utterances can never teach me: "The light is still at the still point of the turning world."

I have felt this touch of the Spirit many times when walking in the woods. The first time this happened to me was at the Trappist monastery of Gethsemani in Kentucky. I found myself bounding down secluded paths, singing loud praise to God, inviting all of creation to join with me. I sang with the birds. I sang with the spring flowers. I sang with the overflowing creeks and laughing spillways. I do not remember the songs I sang, but I am sure God does and holds them, perhaps, as my greatest works of art.

Most often these raptures of tears and silence come in the solitude of my hermitage or in our chapel during the dark, quiet hours before the dawn. Here, I have truly experienced "eternity in an hour." I might completely lose myself for hours, thinking only a few minutes have passed. At other times, I think I have been "caught up" into God for a long time, only to discover I have been praying for two or three minutes at the most. "In the Lord's eyes, one day is as a thousand years and a thousand years are as a day" (2 Pet. 3:8).

These raptures occur when I experience so much of my Lover and my God at once that my mind "short-circuits," allowing my heart to soar free into the realms of eternity. This puny heart and mind of mine can hold only so much of God at a time! But when He graciously reveals so much of His very self to me—not unlike an ocean pouring into a thimble—I am lifted out of myself to what "eye has not seen, ear has not heard," and my spirit comprehends those things which "God has prepared for those who love Him" (1 Cor. 2:9). His glory and His eternity, the gifts "He gives to His beloved in sleep" (Ps. 127:2), are far beyond my human comprehension, let alone my feeble words.

It all comes down to love. He touches me with love, and I respond in love. This mystery is beyond my words. I laugh and I cry. I shout in loud praise, and I am reduced to silence. He removes a veil between us and reveals wonders far to my right and far to my left. The King of Glory has entered into my very soul, and my heart expands to the point of near explosion. I truly believe that were my divine Lover to reveal too much of Himself to me at once, my heart would explode and I would die.

In Paul's second letter to the Corinthians he speaks of a "rapture" where he heard divine truths unable to be repeated. "I must go on boasting, however useless it may be, and speak of visions and revelations of the Lord. I know a man in Christ who, fourteen years ago, whether he was in or outside his body I cannot say, only God can say—a man who was snatched up to third heaven. I know that this man—whether in or outside his body I do not know, God knows—was snatched up to Paradise to hear words which cannot be uttered, words which no man may speak" (2 Cor. 12:1–3). Likewise, some of the things heard by John during his visions recounted in Revelation could not be written down or repeated (Rev. 10:4). So should it surprise us when we ourselves often experience knowledge in the Spirit that cannot be formulated into ideas and words? Yet the knowledge remains active within us intuitively through the presence of the Spirit (Rom. 8:26–27).

I am reminded of the Franciscan hermit and contemporary of St. Francis, Brother John of Alverna, who is said to have experienced such knowledge during a rapture. One story about him says that while first meditating on the humanity of Christ he was overcome by the Spirit and "his soul was drawn out of his body, and his soul and heart were burning a hundred times more than if he had been in a furnace.

"Afterward God raised him above every creature so that his soul was absorbed and assumed into the abyss of the Divinity and Light, and it was buried in the ocean of God's Eternity and Infinity, to the point he could not feel anything that was created or formed or finite or conceivable or visible which the human heart could conceive or the tongue could describe.

"And he felt the eternal infinite love which led the Son of God to incarnate out of obedience to His Father. And by meditating and pondering and weeping on that path of the Incarnation and Passion of the Son of God, he came to unutterable insights."

In another story John is said to have experienced God's presence so strongly during a rapture that "he could not express it in words."

Francis came close to expressing the inexpressible with the streams of praise that fill his writings. Especially in the last chapters of his first Rule, we find Francis expressing the rapture of love in words that bubble forth like water from a fountain, expressing no academic, dry theology, but the spirit of his personal love union with Christ Jesus found in mystical love touch. In his "Letter to All the Faithful" he speaks of this union saying, "On all those who do this and endure to the last the Spirit of God will rest (Is. 11:2), He will make His dwelling in them and there He will stay ... it is they who are the brides, the brothers, and the mothers of our Lord Jesus Christ. A person is His bride when his faithful soul is united with Jesus Christ by the Holy Spirit; we are His brothers when we do the will of His Father in heaven (Mt. 12:50), and we are mothers to Him when we enthrone Him in our hearts and souls by love with a pure and sincere conscience, and give birth to Him by doing good."

St. Bonaventure also speaks of the gifts of rapture and ecstasy in reference to the mysticism of the Lover and Beloved. It almost seems he takes for granted a common consensus of belief in their validity when he says in his book *On the Perfection of Life*, "You will rush into His embrace, will kiss Him with such intimate fervor that you will be completely carried away, wholly enraptured in heaven." In the same work he writes, "The height of devotion may sometimes cause our spirit to lose hold of itself and rise above itself, to pass into a state of rapture when we are inflamed with the ardor of such celestial desire that the whole world seems bitter and tiresome." Also, "Rapture sometimes occurs ... when our soul is irradiated with divine light and, held in suspense by the wonder of the supreme Beauty, it is thrown off its foundation. In the likeness of a flash of lightning, the deeper the soul is cast into the abyss by the contrast between the unseen Beauty and itself, the higher and faster does it rise to the sublime . . . . Once our soul has tasted this intimate abundance of internal sweetness . . . it completely forgets what it is and what it was, and its whole being becomes supernatural desire, carried away as it is in a state of wonderful happiness." Who can doubt that St. Bonaventure won for himself the title of "Seraphic Doctor" by his own experience of the mystical? Would that we all had that title!

Gifts of the Spirit

From all this we can see a great similarity between the Franciscan experience of rapture and the modern experience of the charismatic renewal. In fact, if we look to the early sources on the life of St. Francis we can see almost all of the "gifts of the Spirit" evidenced in Francis and the first brothers, plus a few more that make our modern charismatic experiences seem sober and tame. It is significant that St. Francis calls the Holy Spirit the minister general of the Order.

In the *Omnibus of Sources*, a compilation of writings of and about St. Francis, the excerpts of Bonaventure's sermons and works show us many evidences of the charismatic gifts of the Spirit. Francis was "rapt in ecstasy the time he went to preach in the cathedral. The friars had remained in the hut where they were living and he was about a mile away from them—and he appeared to them in a fiery chariot. Their hearts were bathed in its radiance, so that they could see one another's consciences." Francis's first biographer, Thomas of Celano, speaks of Francis preaching in the Spirit before the pope and the cardinals saying, "He spoke with such great fervor of spirit,

that, not being able to contain himself for joy, he moved
his feet as though he were dancing ... as one burning
with the fire of divine love." Sound familiar? Today we
call this dancing in the Spirit. In another of Bonaventure's
sermons, we see Francis "penetrating hidden secrets and
appearing to those far away. He enjoyed God's illumi-
nating Spirit to the full." Another story speaks of the
"numerous miracles which he worked. He cleansed lepers,
raised the dead, and healed the sick; he restored speech to
the dumb." Francis enjoyed what we now call the word
of knowledge and the gift of prophecy. As Bonaventure
says, "St. Francis had knowledge of what was hidden; he
knew many secrets and could foretell the future."

In Bonaventure's *Minor Life of St. Francis*, these gifts
also appear. "The spirit of the prophets rested upon him,
in all its different forms, with an overflowing abundance
of grace. By its miraculous power the saint often appeared
to those who were far away and knew what went on at a
distance; he could read the secrets of men's hearts and
foretell what the future was to bring." This example of
bilocation certainly reminds us of that scriptural example
found in Acts 8:26–40.

The *Little Flowers of St. Francis* are filled with references to the charismatic works of the Spirit, capturing
most authentically much of the spirit, if not the facts, of
the early brothers. The first chapter gives us a sweeping
overview of the charismatic dimension of the early Franciscans saying, "And just as those holy Apostles were for
the whole world marvels of holiness, filled with the Holy
Spirit, so these most holy companions of St. Francis were
men of such sanctity that the world has not had such wonderful and holy men from the times of the Apostles until
now. For one of them was caught up to third heaven like
St. Paul, and that was Brother Giles. Another—tall Brother
Philip—was touched on the lips by an angel with a burn-

ing coal, like Isaias the Prophet. Another—Brother Sylvester, a very pure and virginal soul—spoke with God as one friend with another, as Moses did. Another, by the keenness of his mind, soared up to the light of divine wisdom, like the eagle (John the Evangelist)—and this was very humble Brother Bernard, who used to explain Holy Scripture in a most profound way. Another was sanctified by God and canonized in Heaven while he was still living in the world, as though he had been sanctified in his mother's womb—and he was Brother Rufino, a nobleman of Assisi and a man most loyal to Christ." These names turn up time and time again in connection with the working of the charismatic gifts of the Spirit.

Bonaventure tells us a story of Francis exercising the great charismatic gift of the desert fathers—discernment of spirits. In this incident, Brother Rufino is deceived by the devil who came to him in the form of the Crucified One and told him not to try so hard to follow Francis because both he and Francis were predestined for damnation. This false apparition also told him not to tell Francis about the vision. "But the Holy Spirit revealed what Brother Rufino did not tell the holy Father." After Francis discerned this evil spirit, he told Rufino to answer the spirit confidently the next time it appeared saying, "Open your mouth and I will empty my bowels in it." Thus it was that Francis exercised the charismatic gift of discernment of spirits, helped Rufino to put the devil to flight, and showed a talent for salty language as well!

Once, when traveling to a town to be treated for his eye sickness, Francis worked a kindly miracle. The crowd that came to meet him was so large that he "turned aside and went to a certain church that was about two miles away from the town." Well, the crowd followed him in their zeal so that "the vineyard of the priest of that church—for it was vintage time—was completely ruined and all the grapes were taken and eaten. When the priest saw the damage, he was bitterly sorry and he regretted that he had allowed St. Francis to go into his church.

"The priest's thoughts were revealed to the Saint by the Holy Spirit." Francis goes on to promise the priest an increase in his normal yield if the priest will let Francis stay on "because of the rest and quiet that I find here," and if the priest will "let everyone take the grapes from this vineyard of yours, for the love of God and my poor little self." On behalf of our Lord Jesus Christ, the fruit of the vineyard was not only saved, but it also multiplied far beyond its normal yield!

The list of stories could go on and on. Words of knowledge, prophecy, healing, discernment of spirits, tongues, levitations, raptures, and power over the elements . . . all are attested to in abundance throughout the early writings. Thomas of Celano speaks of Francis exorcising demons from a whole town by "speaking psalms of praise before the face of God." In Celano's *Treatise on the Miracles of Blessed Francis* we even hear of the dead being raised through Francis's prayers.

I have certainly not been given all these gifts of the Spirit. But, like the little brothers of St. Francis's time, I have witnessed almost all of them actively manifested within the Church of our day. I am sure that most of us have seen or heard similar stories.

I first experienced the gift of rapture and tongues before I knew what they were called. There I was, sitting respectfully on an airplane, gazing at the clouds outside my window. Suddenly overwhelmed by their beauty, I was led to praise their Creator quietly in my heart. I must have been totally overwhelmed. The next thing I knew, I was rousing myself from a kind of trance by singing a spontaneous melody with words from a language I had never heard before. Yet in my spirit I understood perfectly the meaning of those words. It was over a year later that someone finally explained to me I had experienced the gift of rapture and had sung a new song with the gift of tongues. I wish someone could have told the businessman sitting next to me on that flight!

From that time on I became aware of the supernatural work of the Spirit within all members of the Church, and less skeptical to hear that a healing or miracle had taken place in the lives of those around me. I even became more comfortable around those whom previously I had labeled "Jesus Freaks." I was slowly realizing that Jesus doesn't make freaks out of people; He makes people out of freaks.

Now when people tell me of miracles that have occurred during one of my musical meditations, I am apt to believe them. After a concert at South Bend, Indiana, a brother first told me that my music ministry had been for him a deliverance ministry similar to David's, for "whenever the spirit from God seized Saul, David would take the harp and play, and Saul would be relieved and feel better, for the evil spirit would leave him" (1 Sam. 16:23). Since then, many people reported that they have been delivered from evil spirits or have experienced physical healing while listening to my simple music. The beauty of it is that I am totally unaware of these supernatural gifts occurring while I sing. Dorothy Day once said of St. Thérèse of Lisieux, "She told her story and God did the rest." It is the same with me. I sing praise to Jesus my Lover, and He takes care of the rest.

I suppose it is my personal experience that makes me less wary of the quaint Franciscan miracle stories. Some simply write them off as well-meaning exaggerations designed to stir the credulous medieval mind to greater devotion. But after witnessing and experiencing similar manifestations of the Spirit, I do not see these stories as too difficult for God.

So let us continue with a few more of these tales, accepting them with the faith and wonder of little children. "Legends" you may call them, but let's not be too hasty. What became "legend (lej'end) n. 1. An unverified popular story handed down from earlier times" began as the "story of a saint." Can man imagine what God cannot achieve? Then these stories are not impossible for the work of God's Spirit among his simple people. Remember, those who think themselves wise are fools, while those who choose to become fools for Christ will experience the true wisdom of God.

Bonaventure reports how Francis raised Brother Masseo up into the air after being inflamed by the power of the Spirit in prayer. After the two went into a local church as was their custom when entering a town, Francis hid himself behind the altar to pray. He was given a divine vision and visitation that wholly inflamed his soul with such intense longing and love for holy poverty that flames of love seemed to issue from his face and mouth.

"And going out to his companion, all afire with love, he said forcefully: 'Ah! Ah! Ah! Brother Masseo, give yourself to me!'

"And he said it three times. And Brother Masseo, greatly amazed at his fervor, threw himself into the holy father's arms.

"Then St. Francis, with his mouth wide open and repeating very loudly 'Ah! Ah! Ah!,' by the power of the Holy Spirit lifted Brother Masseo up in the air with his breath and projected him forward the length of a long spear."

Bonaventure tells of St. Anthony of Padua who appeared before the pope and the cardinals and "being inflamed by the Holy Spirit and inspired with apostolic eloquence, preached and explained the word of God so effectively . . . that all who were assembled at that consistory, although they spoke different languages, clearly and distinctly heard and understood every one of his words as if he had spoken in each of their languages." This is not unlike the experience of those present at the first Pentecost (Acts 2:1–13): "They were much confused because each one heard these men speaking in his own language."

It is interesting to note that both St. Francis and St. Anthony not only preached to man under the power of the Spirit, but also to animals such as birds and fish. Both saints preached to birds and fish when the people would not listen, as a sign to the people of the power of God's word. Clearly, there were many languages in creation that cannot be spoken by the tongue, but which can be listened to and addressed. So we are reminded by the example of these two saints to invite all creation to praise the Lord, as Jesus well knew it could. "If [my disciples] were to keep silence, I tell you the very stones would cry out" (Lk. 19:40).

The gift of tongues, if not a humorous childlikeness, is also alluded to in Celano's account of Francis's sermon by the manger scene at the hermitage at Greccio. Francis breaks into bleating sounds every time he comes to the word "Bethlehem." Likewise, after picking up a stick from the ground and using it "as though he were playing a viol," he would begin to dance before the Lord singing loud praises to God by bursting into French. Thus it is when the Holy Spirit wells up from inside us so that we must praise God with our tongues, yet we find ordinary human words too limiting for the surge of divine love and inner peace we feel. Thus it was that the early Franciscans spoke in tongues.

There are also stories that portray the brothers as being "slain in the Spirit." This phenomenon occurs when one is so overcome by the peace of the Holy Spirit that he or she simply must lie down . . . one can no longer stand or even sit. While the term "slain in the Spirit" might frighten many people, I think most people of prayer can relate to the experience of this overwhelming peace.

Bonaventure tells of a Brother Simon who also experienced this gift of peace. Brother Simon was a solitary who experienced many graces from God. "He was rarely seen outside his cell. If he sometimes went among the friars, he was always eager to talk about God.

"Thus one evening when he went into the woods with Brother James of Massa to talk about God, they spoke so very sweetly and devoutly about Christ's love that they spent the whole night in that conversation." This must have been some charismatic sharing session!

"This Brother Simon received such consolations from the Holy Spirit that when he felt a divine illumination and visitation of God's love coming over him, he used to lie down on his bed as if he wanted to sleep, because the sweet peace of the Holy Spirit required of him not only mental but also physical rest." Now don't become confused. Taking an afternoon nap is not the same as being slain in the Spirit! But being slain in the Spirit may require of you a "holy nap." Still, I don't suppose that many of us have the grace of knowing ahead of time when we will receive this "visitation of God's love." But lucky Brother Simon could prepare for the inevitable whenever he seriously prayed. He simply went to bed. It probably saved him from many an awkward moment!

From this we can perceive that some of the early Franciscans did, in fact, experience what we now call being "slain in the Spirit" during prayer. When the first brothers once came together to speak spontaneously about God, Francis commanded them all "to say about God whatever the Holy Spirit suggested." Finally, this went on with such power and zeal that "Our Lord Jesus Christ appeared among them in the form of a very handsome young man.

And giving His blessing to all of them, He filled them with such sweet grace that St. Francis as well as all the others were rapt out of themselves, and they lay on the ground like dead men, completely unconscious."

A similar experience happened to Francis and Clare when they ate a meal together at the Portiuncula. "When it was time to eat, St. Francis and St. Clare sat down together.... But at first course St. Francis began to speak about God in such a sweet and holy and profound and divine and marvelous way that he himself and St. Clare and her companions and all the others who were at the poor little table were rapt in God by the overabundance of divine grace that descended upon them.

"And while they were sitting there, in a rapture with their eyes and hands raised to Heaven, it seemed to the men of Assisi ... and the entire district that the Church of St. Mary of the Angels and the whole Place and the forest which was at that time around the Place were all aflame and that an immense fire was burning over all of them. Consequently, the men of Assisi ran down there in great haste to ... put out the fire.

"But when they reached the Place, they saw that nothing was on fire. Entering the Place, they found St. Francis with St. Clare, and all the companions sitting around that very humble table, rapt in God by contemplation and invested with power from on high.

"Later, after a long while, when St. Francis and St. Clare and the others came back to themselves they felt so refreshed by spiritual food that they paid little or no attention to the material food."

This might remind the modern reader of many of the reported experiences of the early "Jesus People" or "Catholic Pentecostals." In the early days of these movements it was not uncommon to hear about prayer meetings where light like fire was seen hovering above and around those rapt in prayer, praise, and worship of Jesus. It is easy to write such experiences off to excessive imaginations, until you begin to see a consistent presence of such phenomenon of the Spirit throughout the history of the Church.

Of course we can also speak of the levitations experienced during rapture. Perhaps the most famous of all stories of Francis's levitations occurred during Leo and Francis's sojourn on Mt. Alverna preceding the miracle of the stigmata. During that intense contemplative retreat we hear how Leo began to realize that something extraordinary was going to happen. "From that time on," says one account of the reception of the holy stigmata, "Brother Leo . . . tried as much as he could to see what the saint was doing. . . . Time and time again he saw St. Francis rapt in God and raised above the ground. He found him outside his cell raised up into the air sometimes as high as three feet, sometimes four, at other times halfway up or at the top of the beech trees—and some of these trees were very high. At other times he found him raised so high in the air and surrounded by such radiance that he could hardly see him."

Being surrounded by "such radiance" can also be seen in the life of St. Seraphim of Sarov, the "St. Francis of the Russian Orthodox." As Raphael Brown in his book *True Joy from Assisi* reports, "Seraphim was a hermit-monk who, like Francis, was popular with both the animals of the forest and the people of the world. Like Francis, he emphasized spiritual joy that comes from being indwelt and filled with the Holy Spirit. At one time while speaking to a man named Motovilov about the Holy Spirit, Seraphim took him firmly by the shoulders, looking him squarely in the eye, and suddenly, the Saint's face began to radiate a blinding light." In the spirituality of the Christian East, this radiance of the Spirit is called the "Taboric Light," because, like Motovilov, through it we share in the glorious mystery of Jesus' transfiguration on Mt. Tabor. "Motovilov said that, instead of being frightened, he felt 'a calm and peace that I cannot express in words . . . an unknown sweetness . . . an unknown joy in my whole heart.'" St. Seraphim is known to say "the Spirit of God turns to joy all that He touches." It is not unlike the story of Brother Masseo quoted earlier, who trusted himself to the human embrace of Francis and received a divine visitation of the Holy Spirit.

Let us end with some wonderful Franciscan stories about Brother John of Alverna who takes us back to the heart of what was said earlier concerning raptures and charismatic gifts. In one story, John is said to be celebrating Mass when he was overcome with rapture and love in the Spirit at the time of the consecration. He tried to continue the Mass but "infusions of divine grace cannot be controlled by human beings." He began to pronounce the words of consecration over the host, but he kept repeating the first half of the formula—*Hoc est—Hoc est*—very often, and was unable to go any further. The reason he could not go on was that he felt and saw the presence of Christ and a throng of angels and saints, so that he almost fainted because of their grandeur which he felt in his soul.

"Therefore, after saying '*Hoc est Corpus Meum*,' he was rapt in an ecstasy and fell backward. . . . He was carried into the sacristy as if he were dead. For his body had turned cold like a corpse. And his fingers were so stiffly contracted that they could hardly be opened or moved. And he lay there unconscious from morning until Terce.

"Among other things he told me that before and while he was consecrating, his heart became liquified like heated wax, and his body seemed to be without bones, so that he could not lift his arms or his hands to make the sign of the cross over the host. And he added that before he became a priest, it was revealed to him that he would faint that way during Mass."

Thus, we see with Brother John of Alverna many of the manifestations of rapture in the Spirit. Note also that Brother John experienced this charismatic gift during the divine liturgy. Here we are reminded of a similar experience that happened to the Jews during the liturgical consecration of Solomon's temple (2 Chron. 5:14). These precedents should encourage us to seek a similar marriage of liturgical form and charismatic freedom during our modern liturgies. It would be easy to write all these things off as delusions or overzealous inventions; we may think they have no place in something as sacred and stately as our celebration of the Eucharist. However, it is usually true that those who have never been thus visited by the Spirit are the ones who try the hardest to disprove their authenticity and prevent their appearance. Those who have experienced some of what is spoken of will usually accept them with proper caution. These will often go on to experience much of what Francis himself experienced on Mt. Alverna.

It is this same John of Alverna who did, in fact, experience much of Francis's charismatic gifts and graces while living as a hermit on Mt. Alverna. In John we see these charismatic experiences centered entirely on the personal love relationship with Jesus Christ offered to us all. In fact, all the early accounts of his life describe his mystical journey in light of the relationship between the Lover and the Beloved. As one beautiful story recounts, he runs after Jesus as an infant after its mother to be nursed. But "now that Brother John was, as we have seen, raised up first to the feet of Christ with tears, then to the hands with graces, and third to the blessed breast with a rapture and rays of light—these are mysteries which cannot be explained in brief words." But let him who wants to understand it read St. Bernard on the Canticle of Canticles; there he describes the successive stages: the beginners at the feet, those progressing to the hands, the perfect who receive the kiss and embrace.

However, with all of our enthusiasm about the charismatic gifts and the raptures and ecstasies of love union, we should exercise some caution. Boniface Maes says in *Franciscan Mysticism*: "Be most careful, then, to avoid giving access to your heart to any curious desire for spiritual gifts, experimental or sensible sweetness, revelations, etc., lest the angel of shadows, finding in this curiosity and self-seeking an open field for his operations, transform himself into an angel of light for your deception."

There are two extremes to be avoided here. One is what is commonly referred to as "spiritual gluttony." An individual can almost lust after the excitement and "spiritual high" of charismatic experiences. While the Beloved should long for union with her Lover, she should not lust after Him, lest the union of this spiritual sexuality become a self-centered, rather than a Christ-centered, intercourse. In order for this union to remain "like Christ," or "Christian," the Bride must abandon herself to her Husband totally for the sake of her Husband, just as Jesus laid down His life for the sake of His Bride. After this mutual death, or giving of self, comes the resurrection of mutually receiving from one another.

The second extreme is to avoid the gift of the charismatic experience which Jesus desires to give you. Many people say "These gifts are good, but they are not for me." Others, thinking themselves spiritually advanced in contemplation, look down long, pharisaical noses at the so-called "beginners" who still need such "crutches" for spirituality. Both of these attitudes indicate subtle, or even blatant, spiritual pride. The first is like a refusal to consummate your marriage, or to hold back from total self-abandonment during sexual intercourse. The other attitude indicates the "spiritual snob" who subtly thinks himself better than the "childish," such as Francis of Assisi or Teresa of Avila. Remember, you who proudly sit back and wait for your Husband to come chasing after you to initiate mystical union, you also must long to be united with Him. It was a dear and whimsical friend who once told me, "God's not so unusual. Like any lover, He likes to be chased." At times we must chase after God and "stir into flame the gift of God" (2 Tim. 1:6).

Summary

We can conclude that this stage of mystical "love touch" between the Lover and the Beloved is an intense emotional and spiritual release, which totally abandons one unto the other in passionate love union. This stage rightly involves the emotions and even the senses in a positive way. This, the stage of mystical union, this spiritual sexuality, flows almost unnoticeably from the previous stage of "dialogue" with Jesus, or meditation which rightly involves the whole person. Yet for the involvement of the emotions and senses to be holy they must be totally selfless, as when a husband and wife give themselves to one another in sexual intercourse even as Christ gave Himself for the Church and the Church gives herself for Jesus. When this total abandonment of self is given for the other, then great charismatic gifts and consolations of the Spirit are given freely by Jesus to His Bride. In this He totally impregnates the human soul with the gift of His divine and Holy Spirit, even as a husband impregnates the womb of his Beloved with the seed of his very life. In this, we the Bride will always carry the life of Jesus within the womb of our own life.

4
AFTERGLOW

✤

For sensitive husbands and wives the time immediately after sexual union is often precious. It is a time of silence, a time of stillness. It is a time of profound fulfillment and peace. A time to simply be with each other.

To try and speak too much during this special time would be to invade upon the profound intimacy of its silence. To try and make love again would be to trade the full quality of this precious union in exchange for a superficial copy as if it could be reproduced liked a cheap painting. The silent tenderness of this "afterglow" is something to savor, like the taste of the finest of wines. It is a time for lovers simply to rest in each other's arms and be, knowing that they have become one body in a way no other human exchange can rival.

The same holds true in our love relationship with Jesus. After we have dialogued with Him through meditation and become one with Him through charismatic rapture and ecstasy, it is a time simply to learn how to be with Jesus. It is no longer a time to meditate or study scripture, nor is it a time to try and artificially stir up the charismatic gifts. It is a time to simply be still and know the Lord your God.

Many Christians get very confused when they come to

this point in their love relationship with Christ. Because they are so used to constant action and motion in their Christian life, they think that something must be wrong if all they experience is silence and stillness in their prayer life. They are so accustomed to stimulating times of scripture studies and meditations, they think something must be wrong when they seem to get nothing from the now familiar verses. Some are so used to experiencing the thrill of charismatic prayer that they think something must be blocking the flow of the Spirit when no charismatic phenomenon or feeling of excitement occurs during their prayer time.

Actually, there is usually nothing wrong at all! In fact, everything is often so fine that Jesus is simply calling you on to yet another level or stage of relationship with Him. The best thing to do at this point is nothing. Simply relax and quit struggling. Once you relax the Spirit can move you easily into this stage of spiritual afterglow where you can learn how to just be and rest in the arms of your divine Lover. It is a time so precious that, once you experience its profound peace, you will realize that this is, in many ways, the crowning completion of the previous mystical levels in your relationship with Jesus.

Unknowing and Darkness

It is with the experience of this level of prayer that the soul passes from meditation and charismatic rapture to the deeper and more mysterious treasures of what we call "the contemplative life." Up until now we have rightly sought the positive movement of our imagination and our emotions, but now we must give all these things up for a time to learn the contemplative way of simply "being" in the sacred presence of God. It happens when the inner and the outer man become one, when we really *know* that we "live and move and have our being in Him" (Acts 27:28). It is a special kind of knowing in which we cease to know at all!

St. John of the Cross speaks of this stage of "unknowing" when he writes in his poetry:

> *I entered into unknowing*
> *Yet when I saw myself there*
> *Without knowing where I was*
> *I understood great things;*
> *I shall not say what I felt*
> *For I remained in unknowing*
> *Transcending all knowledge.*

As the author of *The Cloud of Unknowing* says, "A man may know completely and ponder thoroughly every created thing and its works, yes, and God's works too, but not God Himself. Thought cannot comprehend God. Though we cannot know Him we can love Him. By love He may be touched and embraced, never by thought."

Of course he concedes that it is good to think about God, but, "in real contemplative work you must set all thinking aside and cover it over with a 'cloud of forgetting.' Then let your loving desire . . . step bravely and joyfully beyond it and reach out to pierce the darkness above. Yes, beat upon that thick 'cloud of unknowing' with the dart of your loving desire and do not cease come what may."

St. John of the Cross often uses the language of "divine darkness" to describe the unsearchable love mysteries of our infinite God, and uses the theme of the Lover and the Beloved as the reason to enter this dark night of the soul.

> *O guiding night!*
> *O night more lovely than the dawn!*
> *O night that has united*

The Lover with His Beloved,
Transforming the Beloved in her Lover.

He then speaks of the "afterglow" which the divine darkness has brought through the "dark night":

> *Upon my flowering breast,*
> *Which I kept wholly for Him alone,*
> *There He lay sleeping,*
> *And I caressing Him*
> *There in a breeze from the fanning cedars*
> *I abandoned and forgot myself,*
> *Laying my face on my Beloved;*
> *All things ceased; I went out from myself,*
> *Leaving my cares*
> *Forgotten among the lilies.*

This kind of language can indeed be very confusing for the average Christian. We might rightly ask "If Jesus is the light of the world, why all this talk of darkness?" Or, "Jesus says we will know the truth and the truth will set us free, so why all this talk of unknowing?" Granted, we are to "test the spirits," and many angels of darkness have come as angels of light, but I must confess that when I first heard this kind of language in connection with relationship with Jesus, I too suspected that the enemy was coming in the Lord's name to try and destroy the Light of God with the darkness of confusion.

The scriptures are full of this language of "unknowing." Even though God's nature is revealed through the many stories of the Old and New Testaments, it is still true that "now we see indistinctly, as in a mirror" (1 Cor. 13:12). What remains partially unknown to us—for who can know the mind of God—is the Father, revealed continually through the Son. As Hans Urs von Balthasar writes, "The word of Jesus sounds from out of a place of silence. . . . That place is, firstly, the silence of the Father, 'who has revealed Himself through His Son, Jesus Christ, who is His Word come forth from silence.'" A perfect example is the story of the transfiguration. Here the light of Jesus is the bright and glorious symbol indicating He is the revelation of the Father. "This is my beloved Son. Listen to Him." At the same time, He is surrounded by the great and mysterious cloud of the Father, who chooses to remain unknown in Himself, hidden in yet emanating from the incarnation. This symbol of "unknowing" actually speaks of God's infinity and awesome transcendence, or "otherliness." Even St. Bonaventure, who advocated finding God in and through creation, says that the hiddenness of God expresses His transcendence. "For instance, we say, 'God . . . is above the senses; nor is He imaginable, intelligible, manifest, but is above all these concepts. . . . As Denis says, 'affirmations are inadequate. . . . Negations seem to say less but actually say more.'" In all of this "our vision of truth must be elevated toward the incomprehensible."

In other words, what we can rightly say about God is next to nothing when compared to what we do not yet know about God. God is infinite, therefore we can often say more about Him by saying what we do not know, rather than what we know. In this we can often say more about God by our silence than we can by our words. This is paradox, yet it is true.

Our God is a God of paradox for our God is a God of mystery. Our God is a God of mystery because He is a God of love, and love exceeds all logic. Therefore, we can often best speak of the truth of our God by speaking in paradoxes.

A paradox is a seeming contradiction that remains true. An example would be to say that God is everywhere, yet He is nowhere. This statement speaks directly to our heart of God's omnipresence and God's infiniteness. It seems to defy the logic of the human mind, yet it speaks intuitively to the human heart of an eternal truth. We are here reminded of scripture that says: "My thoughts are not your thoughts" (Is. 55:8–9).

These paradoxes also apply directly to Jesus who is, in fact, the ultimate manifestation of paradox. In Jesus we can say that we must look upon the human to understand the divine, and we must look upon the divine to understand the human. In Jesus we can say that God's glory is revealed in humility; His wealth and riches in poverty; His healing in one who was bruised and broken. We can, of course, see the ultimate paradox manifested in the cross, where Jesus teaches us that we can only come to live forever by continually dying to ourselves. The paradox of Jesus takes us into the seeming heights of even the marvelous paradoxes that bring Buddhist "enlightenment," yet they take us much further beyond in the paradox of finding the richness of personal love relationship in the midst of our "nothingness."

So it is with the language of "unknowing" and divine "darkness." Paradoxically, we can only come to "know" God when we enter into this unknowing, and we can only gaze directly into the fullness of God's incomprehensible "light" when we enter into the darkness. Thus it was that Jesus had to enter the darkness and unknowing of the tomb before He could pass over into resurrection. In this we, the beloved Bride of Christ, come to experience intimately the living paradox of our Lover.

Even with these explanations it remains very difficult to shed any light on the experience of divine darkness. It is very difficult to speak about silence with words or share the sacredness of solitude with a crowd. How can I relate imageless prayer with an image, or a love union that exceeds thoughts and concepts with an intelligible thought? If I have succeeded it probably indicates I have failed.

St. Bonaventure writes of the afterglow period between the Lover and the Beloved in these words: "If this passing over is to be perfect, all intellectual operations must be given up.... Such a motion as this is something mystical and very secret, and no one knows it except him who receives it, and no one receives it except him who desires it, and no one desires it unless the fire of the Holy Spirit ... inflames him to the very marrow." How similar to the scriptures' own teachings reflected so clearly in the words of John the Baptist, who was firm in his conviction that "no one can lay hold on anything unless it is given him from on high" (Jn. 3:27). Bonaventure too considers the "passing over" into the divine darkness of unknowing as a gift of the Spirit. Bonaventure was no stranger to Paul either, who wrote that "no one knows a man's innermost self but the man's own spirit within him" (1 Cor. 2:11), words almost identical to the above phrase, "... and no one knows it except him who receives it." Indeed, it is true that those who have not yet received this gift from the Spirit simply will not understand the way of contemplation. They will consider such ultimate paradox as foolish as the cross itself (1 Cor. 1:18; 2:6, 7, 10).

Martha and Mary

I have found that I am often misunderstood when speaking of this contemplative way. Just as Martha complained to Jesus about Mary, so many active Christians complain about the contemplatives of the Church. Many people write to me and ask what I really accomplish from this mountain hermitage, when the "real" world perishes in social and spiritual darkness. Of course I could point to the sacred music I compose from the "conservatory of silence,"

the pages I fill with words after experiencing the empti-
ness of the cross, the concerts and other fund-raising activities done to raise money for the poor. I could point to the
seemingly countless people who have been touched by
Christ through my ministry because I first learned to find
Christ in the midst of my solitude. In this sense, my own
experience of divine darkness in contemplative prayer
helps bring people to the light of Christ through my active
ministry. Without these active ministries being "pruned"
by the discipline of solitude and silence, they would never
be truly fruitful.

However, I would rather follow the beautiful lead of
Thérèse of Lisieux, for her "little way" makes no attempt
to justify the effectiveness of a vocation to prayer in terms
of her own activity. In her mind, contemplatives are the
heart of the Body of Christ. The heart is unseen to the light
of the outer world, yet without it the whole body dies. The
heart pumps the lifeblood to the hands and feet, yet the
heart remains hidden in the darkness. Her view emphasizes
the mystical and practical beauty of diversity and unity in
the Body of Christ. If one part of the Body works, we all
glory in its accomplishment. If one part of the Body prays,
we are all strengthened in the Spirit. Her understanding is
highly mystical, yet it is a "practical mysticism" that helps
us to live in Christ's peace as we seek to live out our individual vocations in harmony, "so that with one heart and
voice you may glorify God, the Father of our Lord Jesus
Christ" (Rom. 15:6).

Nonetheless, it is still my experience that the Marthas
and the Marys of the Church continue to bicker and quib-
ble. I believe this often happens when we take our eyes off
Jesus and focus too narrowly on our own call. Martha
thinks Mary should do some of the work. Mary thinks herself spiritually superior to the active and mundane Martha.
It is not so much that we are called to be like Martha or

Mary. We are called to be like Christ. It is by focusing our eyes on Jesus, who was both active and contemplative, that Martha and Mary can make peace.

It is easy to see why many people do not understand the "unknowing" and divine darkness of the contemplative life. It looks like foolishness and a waste of precious time. We should not, however, be upset by their criticisms, for unless the Holy Spirit reveals the awesome truth of this paradox they cannot know it. In fact, we should rejoice in criticism, for it keeps us humble. Furthermore, sometimes criticism rightly speaks against a holy leisure that has degenerated into idleness and pleasure, and a holy silence that has become a way to escape reality.

The Cloud of Unknowing would say "those striving to be contemplative should not only pardon all who complain about them, but be so occupied with their own work that they do not even notice what is said or done around them." This reminds us of the approach of St. Francis who made it "his greatest concern to be free of everything in this world, lest the serenity of his mind be disturbed.... He made himself insensible to all external senses . . . he occupied himself with God alone."

Celano writes similarly, "Francis was often suspended in such sweetness of contemplation that caught up out of himself he could not reveal what he had experienced because it went beyond all human comprehension." His language here is not unlike that of "knowing" and "unknowing." In fact, one story told by Celano shows just how completely Francis could be rapt in unknowing. Once on a journey, the saint passed through the city of Borgo San Sepolcro when the Lord visited him as he prayed. He kept on, however, straight through the crowds of the men and women who had gathered to see him. Celano writes that "they touched him and pulled him about and cut off little pieces of his tunic to keep" but "the man seemed insensible to all these things, and paid no attention as though he were a lifeless corpse." When he and his companions at last reached their destination, Francis quite sincerely asked when they would reach the city he had expected to pass through!

For Francis, this insensibility was the freedom found in dying to self. "Take a lifeless body and place it where you will . . . it does not resist being moved, it does not murmur about its position, it does not cry out if it is allowed to lie there. . . . He does not ask to be moved, he cares not where he is placed, he does not insist on being changed elsewhere." Celano talks about this same freedom in his reports on the first brothers. "Because they had nothing, loved nothing, they feared in no way to lose anything. . . . They were, therefore, everywhere secure, kept in no suspense by fear, distracted by no care, they awaited the next day without solicitude, nor were they in anxiety. . . ."

However, Francis was neither insensible nor passive when it came to actively following Jesus who taught us to bless those who persecute us (Mt. 5:39, 44). In fact, Francis once told Brother Leo that perfect joy is found only in persecution! "Above all the graces and gifts of the Holy Spirit . . . is that of conquering oneself and willingly enduring sufferings, insults, humiliations, and hardships for the love of Christ." We should remember, as Francis did, that it is those who persecute and blame us who lead us to Christ for they teach us to love.

True and False Contemplatives

Brother Boniface Maes, however, speaks of the rivalry between the contemplatives and the active people of the world as sometimes being the fault of the contemplatives. "Hence comes the opinion, which among certain 'active' souls has become a sort of axiom, 'that contemplatives

ordinarily despise the active,' because they think the contemplative life is more perfect than that of others.... The
accusation is true of imperfect contemplatives, but not of
the perfect, for as the more perfect receive these gifts the
more humble they become."

In several of his Admonitions to the brothers, Francis
warns against false contemplatives and teaches what are
the signs of true contemplatives. "There are many people
who spend all their time at their prayers.... But if anyone
says as much as a word that implies a reflection on their
self-esteem ... they are immediately up in arms and an-
noyed. These people are not really poor in spirit." However, the true contemplative will remain at peace even
when criticized. "They are truly peacemakers who are able
to preserve their peace of mind and heart for love of our
Lord Jesus Christ, despite all that they suffer in the world."
He also says, "Blessed the religious who has no more regard
for himself when people praise him and make much of him
than when they despise him and say that he is ignorant.
What a man is before God, that he is and no more." And in
another Admonition: "A man ... has the Spirit of God if
his lower nature does not give way to pride when God accomplishes some good through him, and if he seems all the
more worthless and inferior to others in his own eyes." So,
a contemplative who walks in humility will not lose his
peace when criticized.

Concerning the criticism of idleness among contemplatives: Yes, Francis hated idleness, for he himself "made his
whole time a holy leisure" during which to pray. It is no
wonder, then, that this man who lived his own ideals to
the fullest "rebuked with no small severity those who lived
in a different manner [than that of the ideal hermitage]
in the hermitages. "For," Celano writes, "many change
the place of contemplation into a place of idleness and
change the eremetical way of life ... into a cesspool of

pleasure." Celano was personally concerned for the abuses he saw among the hermits who lived after the time of Francis's death. "The norm of such hermits of the present time is to live as each one pleases. . . . Would that the hermits of our time would not fall away from the primitive beauty" envisioned by Francis and lived as so many of the early brother/ hermits who "bloomed as solitary flowers." It is significant that the holy hermits described by Celano as the ideal are true to Francis's ideal set down in his Rule for Hermitages, for "half of them take care of domestic needs and the other half spend their time in contemplation. In this way each week those who lead the active life exchange with those who lead the contemplative life." The early Franciscan hermitages reveal many ways in which a balanced rhythm between contemplation and action can be maintained and destructive idleness curtailed.

The saint's intolerance of false silence is revealed also in another story about a hermit of the Order. "Once there was a brother who led a holy and exemplary life: He gave himself over to prayer night and day and observed silence so strictly that when he went to confession . . . he did so by signs, without saying a word. . . . To all appearances he was full of piety and fervent love of God. . . . All were inclined to look upon him as a saint. When Francis learned of his way of acting he said, 'You may be sure that if he does not want to confess his sins, this is a temptation and a trick of the Devil . . . this man is lead and seduced by an evil spirit.'" When finally the silent brother was asked to go to confession, he "put a finger to his lips and shook his head, showing by gestures that he would do nothing of the kind." The story has it that the silent man left the Order and died an unhappy death.

Francis was well aware of the false contemplative syndrome that breeds spiritual pride and illusion rather than an encounter with Christ which nurtures humility. If one is a true contemplative, humility brings him or her joyfully into occasional contact with the business and noise of the world. Rather than seeing them as intrusions on our solitude and silence, we should see them as opportunities for grace.

Distractions in Contemplation

St. Bonaventure speaks of this even purer imageless contemplation in *The Journey of the Mind to God* by quoting Denis the Areopagite: "In regard to mystical visions, with your course now well determined, forsake sense perception and discursive reasoning, all things visible and invisible, every nonbeing and every being; and . . . be restored, naked of knowledge, to union with the very One who is above all created essence and knowledge. Thus . . . unencumbered . . . you will rise to the superessential radiance of divine darkness."

This all sounds very fine, especially for the would-be mystic. But the fact still remains that most of us ordinary Christians have a very difficult time just concentrating on a positive image of Jesus without distracting worldly thoughts, much less clearing our minds of images all together! While this might indicate that we are not yet ready for pure contemplative prayer, take heart; even "seasoned pros" have problems with good and bad images that arise during contemplative prayer. Even St. Francis once smashed a vase he had constructed to battle idleness because he kept thinking about the vase during prayer. How can we deal with these thoughts and images?

In *The Cloud of Unknowing* we hear of a helpful tool in handling such distractions: "When distracting thoughts annoy you, try to pretend that you do not even notice their presence. . . . Look beyond them—over their shoulder, as it were—as if you were looking for something else, which of course you are. For beyond them, God is hidden in the dark cloud of unknowing."

Francis used a similar "visualization" tool to deal with the blatant temptations of the devil that filled his mind during contemplative prayer. While most of Francis's distractions are spoken of as "temptations of the devil," the principles he applied can often be used to deal with both good and bad distracting thoughts during prayer. In one instance, after a temptation had afflicted him in prayer for several years, the Lord told him to picture the temptation as a mountain that could easily be removed even by a little faith. The Lord said, "Francis, if you have faith like a mustard seed, you will say to this mountain, remove from here and it will remove (Mt. 17:19). . . . Francis said, 'Let it be done unto me, Lord, as you have said.' Immediately all temptation was driven out."

Another time, Francis was so besought by sexual temptations that no matter what method he tried, he could not free himself from lust. Finally, after building a family of snow people that represented the family brought forth from sexual intercourse, Francis calmed down and simply thought about the kind of responsibility that goes with family life. Upon considering the real consequences of his sexual desire, he was freed from lust and temptation.

From these examples you can see that one of the best things to do when vain thoughts or images fill your mind while trying to enter into the imageless prayer of contemplation is simply to relax and calm yourself. It is not the end of the world just because you have a few distracting thoughts at prayer. Nor is it something that we don't all go through. The best thing to do is relax and know that the same thing happens to everybody, yet most of us seem to make it. If we faithfully realize that we are in Christ, and submit even our temptations to Him, they will often disappear. The more attention we give to these thoughts, the stronger they will become. The more we passively ignore them, like a schoolyard pest, the more they will go away.

The worst that can happen is that they will continue, causing us to suffer like Christ on the Cross, and since we should not run from this, we should, like St. Francis, simply relax and trust in God. If at times we seem forsaken like Jesus in the garden, it is then we are closest to Jesus crucified.

It is interesting to note that Brother Boniface observes in *Franciscan Mysticism* that the passage into the imageless prayer of the contemplative life occurs "by an almost natural tendency." As St. Bonaventure said, "Such a motion as this is something mystical and secret, and no one knows it . . . unless the fire of the Holy Spirit . . . inflames him." Thus, we can see that the passage over into the "afterglow" of contemplative prayer is a natural flow of the Spirit, once the soul has been impregnated by the Spirit during the spiritual intercourse of rapturous love union with Christ. It cannot be forced.

We can see, therefore, that we need to make sure that the various stages of our love relationship with Jesus are environmentally prepared and protected, both within ourselves, through a Spirit-controlled mind, and without ourselves, through a disciplined asceticism and life-style. But we should not get hung up about methods and techniques of contemplative prayer.

If we are in the Spirit of our Lover, then we can relax and let the specifics of our love union unfold and flow naturally. We cannot mechanically go through the stages of prayer, lest the analogy of the Lover and the Beloved be cheapened and made more to resemble intercourse with a paid prostitute or whore. Nor can we force these stages, lest our gentle love union with Jesus take on the nature of spiritual rape. We should allow our soul to move naturally in the Spirit from meditation to the passionate touch of love union, and from the passionate touch of love union to the gentle stillness and contemplative calm of "afterglow."

Francis understood this. He was not hung up with prayer techniques and detailed accounts on how to chart our course through the mysterious and deep waters of contemplative prayer. He sought only to be in love with Jesus. He loved to talk to Jesus through meditation. He loved to "make love" with Jesus in charismatic rapture. He also loved simply to be with Jesus in the "afterglow" of contemplation. He sought to make each encounter with his Lover a special and precious thing, but he never sought to force Jesus into one expression or the other. He just wanted to live with Jesus, even as a bride longs to share her whole life with the husband she loves. As Thomas of Celano so beautifully says of St. Francis, he was "not so much praying as becoming himself a prayer."

So, concerning distractions, we should relax in the arms of Jesus and make even our distractions opportunities for prayer. Of course, make a reasonable effort to establish a discipline, but if the images of Jesus continue persistently, we should often just relax and enjoy them. If the thoughts are evil, rejoice in the opportunity to join intimately with Jesus crucified who on the cross bore the assault of Satan, battled him, and defeated him. If, after a reasonable attempt to control these thoughts, they continue, it simply means that God might want you to work a little more on meditation rather than contemplation. I am reminded of the approach of St. Peter of Alcantara who said, "We are not so bound down . . . as to think it wrong to pass on . . . to some other subject in which we find more devotion . . . . Nevertheless, we should not avail ourselves of the liberty for any light cause." Remember, meditation and contemplation are both prayer, and even the most advanced contemplatives still use meditation. The most important thing is just to pray and know Jesus Christ.

Summary

Most of us have one of two reactions to the possibility of experiencing "afterglow." Either we are afraid simply to be with Jesus, or we wish to take a short-cut to what we believe is the highest form of prayer available. To those who fear, have courage! Let your times of "dialogue" lead you to trust, and let trust lead you to rapture. Then, having known His love, your fears will be healed. Having experienced and known your Lover through trust, know that He leads you into the unknowing of the darkness to love you even further. It is a time to let go and trust, not to clutch and grasp in doubt. To those who are impatient, be careful you are not motivated by a subtle anxiety to be better than "mere meditators." The stages of prayer are not a matter of "inferior" and "superior," "better than" and "worse than." It is a progression in humility, and we must see the importance of submitting to this beautiful and natural process of growth in our love relationship with the Beloved. So, trembling in your boots or champing at the bit, take to heart Bonaventure's stirring words on contemplative prayer: "If you wish to know how such things come about, consult grace, not doctrine; desire, not understanding; prayerful groaning, not studious reading; the Spouse, not the teacher; God, not man; darkness, not clarity. Consult not light, but the fire that completely inflames the mind and carries it over to God in transports of fervor and blazes of love. This fire is God. . . .

"Let us die, then, and pass over into the darkness; let us silence every care, every craving, every dream; with Christ crucified, let us pass out of this world to the Father (Jn. 13:1)," for Jesus "is to be adored by sacrifice and praise . . . admired in ecstasy and contemplation . . . and embraced with caresses of love." Jesus is to be loved.

Contemplation, quite simply, is the "afterglow" stage of our personal love relationship with Jesus Christ. Now we can rest and be at peace as a bride in the arms of her husband, knowing that we have become totally one through the charismatic rapture and ecstasy of mystical "love union." We can also rest and be at peace knowing that we have "dialogued" with this Lover and therefore know who it is to whom we have just given our body, soul, and spirit. There is nothing left to do now but simply rest in each other's arms and be at peace in the intimate silence and gentle stillness of those precious moments of afterglow. Nurture these moments and savor them. Soon you will drift off to sleep in the secure arms of your divine Lover, knowing that He will pour out His gifts on you His Beloved, even while you slumber (Ps. 127:2; 121:4).

5
DAILY LIFE

❖

With the coming of the dawn the Lover and the Beloved rise to greet the new day, and with that day come the many responsibilities of raising the family of God. The Lover and the Beloved have come to know about each other through "dialogue"; they have come to experience passionately the mystical knowing of each other through "love union," and they have come to learn how to just rest and be with each other through "afterglow." From this whole dynamic process of spiritually making love, the Bride of Christ has been impregnated by the Spirit. After growing fat in the fruit of the Spirit, the Bride has spiritually given birth to the children of Christ. These children are the converts we bring forth into the Church of Jesus Christ, or the family of God.

We can learn much about this new stage in our love relationship with Jesus by looking into the traditional routine of daily life for the wife and mother of a family. The average day begins early with the intruding sound of the alarm clock. In many cases, the woman barely has time to get herself out of bed before she hears the cries of her baby. Usually there are dirty diapers to be changed before the baby can be nursed again. (Sometimes the mother has also had to get up not too many hours before for a midnight feeding.) Then there is breakfast that needs to be prepared.

Of course, for the more mature husband and wife there are other children brought forth from their many love unions. These children, too, must be roused from sleep and gotten ready for school. She sees that they are properly dressed and fed before they go out to meet the bus. Suddenly the husband gets up from the breakfast table and leaves for work to do his share in supporting this growing family, often leaving the wife alone to clean up after this hectic morning ritual and make sure the kids are safely on their way. Just as things begin to settle down, the wife and mother realizes the day has just begun, and the demands of the infant and the younger kids are still to be faced before the rest of the evening.

It would be easy for the wife to feel deserted by her husband at this point. He leisurely rose from sleep and cleaned up while she was hurriedly preparing the family's breakfast. Immediately after eating, he darted off for work, leaving her to clean up the mess left from the activity of the morning. On the surface, she could easily think this unfair.

She can only be reassured by faithfully reminding herself that her husband is also slaving away at work for the good of the whole family. Likewise, she sometimes experiences assurance when reminded of a night they gave themselves to each other and how even in his seeming absence, his seed of life was present and growing in her womb. Furthermore, she is reassured by knowing that he will return again at the end of the day to help her with the love responsibilities of the family and once more to hold her in his arms and join with her in mystical love.

So it is in our relationship with Jesus and the Church. We have risen from sleep to meet the responsibilities of the family of God. There are the spiritually newborn to help cleanse of their past life-styles and to nurse with the milk of the word (1 Cor. 3:1–4; Heb. 5:12, 13). We must also minister to the growing children of God who are advancing toward spiritual maturity (Heb. 5:14–6:3; 1 Cor. 2:6–10). In the midst of all this Jesus has left us seemingly alone (Acts 1:9). Yet by faith (2 Cor. 5:7) we know that He now sits at God's right hand for the sake of the well-being of the family (Rom. 8:34; 1 Jn. 2:1). Also, by faith, we know that we have spiritually made love with our Husband, and that even though we now seem alone, His seed of life has impregnated our innermost spiritual womb through the giving of His Spirit (Gal. 5:22–25). Furthermore, by faith, we know that our Husband will return to hold us forever in the security of His loving embrace and wipe away our every tear (Mt. 24 and 25; Rev. 3:11–12; 21 and 22). So it is that even through the burdens of raising the family (2 Cor. 4:7–5:10) the Beloved continues to cry out in rapturous love for her Lover (Rev. 22:17, 20).

We can see from this that the final stage of our love relationship with Jesus in this age requires a highly integrated and mature mix between the mystical dimensions of prayer and the practical dimensions of active ministry. Scripture portrays the great saints as individuals who understood and embodied this mixed life. Almost all the Church fathers attest to the perfection of this mixed life and lived it themselves as they, too, sought to be good parents to the spiritual children of mother Church. Likewise, almost the whole body of early Franciscan sources portray even the hermit-friars as striving toward the perfection of this way of life.

Prayer and Action

When answering the question as to which is better, the active or the contemplative life, Brother Boniface Maes says, "Considered in itself, the contemplative life is better and more perfect than the active. . . . But the mixed life is preferable to the state of those who only lead the contemplative life . . . these are they, who giving themselves to contemplation of heavenly things, when they have drawn thence light and strength, turn to others to instruct them in doctrine, to dispense the sacraments and to communicate to their neighbor those truths which they have discovered in contemplation."

He goes on with a beautiful lesson from scripture. "We may say that this mixed life was represented in the house of Martha by Christ Himself. . . . Martha has the least part, Mary has chosen the better; but Christ took both. . . . And so those who perfectly follow Christ have not a part but the whole, for not content with contemplation they share their contemplation with others."

The "mixed life" rightly integrates both contemplation and action into a creative and life-giving whole. Our life should be like a cup that overflows to give drink to the thirsty. But a cup must sit still and take the time to be filled before it can overflow. An empty or half-filled cup simply cannot overflow. Our ministries, therefore, must flow from prayer and lead people back to prayer, for it is in prayer that we experience our personal love relationship with Jesus Christ.

Our contemplative life is like an oasis in the desert, and our ministries are like canteens that we fill with living water to give drink to the stranded people of the desert who are dying of thirst. Upon initially refreshing these people from our canteens we must lead them back to the oasis to drink from the source of the living water themselves.

Unless we ourselves begin in the oasis, we cannot fill up our canteens. Furthermore, if we venture away from the oasis too far into the desert for too long, we will not have enough water in our canteens to see us or those to whom we have ministered safely back to the oasis of living water. Then we could both die.

This simple analogy teaches us several things. We must begin our ministry by first becoming mature people of prayer. Our own prayer life must never run dry because of too much time spent in ministry. Thus, a well-planned and healthy balance between contemplation and action will enable us to lead those to whom we minister back to the contemplative life with us. If we do this we will fulfill the demands of both the active and the contemplative lives, integrating them creatively into the healthy balance of the mixed life.

The more scholars study the life of St. Francis, the more they see how he himself did this. Many think that Francis spent as much as seventy-five percent of his time pursuing the contemplative life within the hermitage. We know that during his short religious "career" he still managed to found over twenty-five hermitages within the wooded hills and mountains of Italy. From this we can see that contemplative prayer was always the priority for Francis, but it was from this life of prayer that his powerful ministry naturally overflowed.

We know that the hermitages served as centers for Franciscan ministry. As Cardinal Jacques de Vitry says in his letter of 1216, "During the day they go into the cities and villages, giving themselves over to the active life of the apostolate; at night they return to their hermitage or withdraw into solitude to live the contemplative life." The Portiuncula was the hermitage where all brothers were received into the Order and from which all active missions were sent out. The hermitage at Greccio was the scene of the first Christmas manger scene, to which Francis summoned all the people in the true spirit of evangelization. Poggio Bustone is not only where Francis prayed what became the "Franciscan Jesus Prayer," but also where he developed his famous greeting—"May the Lord give you peace!"—which became the cornerstone of the whole Franciscan peace movement. It was in the solitude of San Damiano that Francis received the commission from Christ to "rebuild my house." Finally, it was in the eremitical solitude of Mt. Alverna that Francis was stigmatized with the marks of Jesus crucified, a miracle that would build the faith of people throughout the world for centuries to come. From this we see that the brothers' active apostolate was rooted and grounded in an intentional life of contemplative prayer.

It is also known that within the hermitage itself the brothers lived the "mixed life" between contemplation and action. In the so-called "Rule for Hermits" Francis says that some of the brothers are to live the contemplative life of Mary, and some of them are to lead the active life of Martha. The "Marthas" are to act as mothers, and the "Marys" are to act as sons. This means that the "mothers" are to be about the domestic chores of the hermitage, while the contemplative "sons" are to be left free to pray. In this, the active "mothers" protect and serve the contemplative "sons." Then Francis spontaneously says, "Now and then the sons should exchange places with the mothers, according to whatever arrangement seems best suited for the moment." In this Francis establishes the Spirit-led rhythms of the "mixed life" for every brother of the hermitage in a way that defies legalism. Here Francis stays true to the spirit of the gospel of Jesus Christ, whose way to greater than either Martha's or Mary's, but includes them both.

In Thomas of Celano's first biography, he speaks of how Francis accomplished this mix of contemplation and action in his own life saying, "He . . . frequently chose solitary places so that he could direct his mind completely to God; yet he was not slothful about entering into the affairs of his neighbors, when he saw the time was opportune, and he willingly took care of things pertaining to their salvation." He goes on to show how he had to make prayer a priority, "For his safest haven was prayer; not prayer of a single moment, or idle or presumptuous prayer, but prayer of long duration." He suggests that involvement in ministry might disturb the exact time schedule, but it should not keep us from the actual commitment to pray. "If he began late, he would scarcely finish before morning." He concludes by speaking not only of a "mixed life," but of a "synthesized life" where prayer and activity became one, saying, "Walking, sitting, eating, or drinking, he was always intent upon prayer." In this we see that Francis no longer saw a separation between contemplation and action. For Francis his whole life was a prayer.

We see this same point made in the second biography of Thomas of Celano. "He made his whole time a holy leisure in which to inscribe wisdom in his heart. . . . When visits of secular persons or any other business disturbed him, he would interrupt his prayers rather than end them and return to them again in his innermost being.

"When he suddenly felt himself visited by the Lord in public, lest he be without a cell he made a cell of his mantle. . . . When he did not have a mantle, he would cover his face with his sleeve. . . . Always he put something between himself and the bystanders, lest they should become aware of the Bridegroom's touch. Thus he could pray unseen even among many people in the narrow confines of a ship." Francis clearly sought to integrate and synthesize ceaseless prayer (1 Thess. 5:17) with action without flaunting his prayer in public like the hypocrites (Mt. 6:5–6). In this regard, Thomas of Celano continues, "Because he was forgetful of himself, there were no sobs or sighs; because he was absorbed in God, there was no hard breathing or external movement." Yet we don't see Francis compromising the zeal and the fire of the Spirit in his moderation. "The blessed father was accustomed not to pass over any visitation of the Spirit with negligence . . . . When, therefore, while he was pressed by some business or was intent upon a journey, he felt little by little certain touches of grace . . . in frequent snatches. For also along the way, with his companions going on ahead, he would stand still, and turning the new inspiration to fruitfulness, he would not 'receive the grace in vain'" (2 Cor. 6:1–2). Here we see the way in which Francis sought out prayer in the Spirit even while on a journey, and how that inspiration of prayer brought forth fruit in the apostolic work of the journey.

Again we see the concept of Francis's life becoming a prayer when Celano says, "All his attention and affection he directed with his whole being . . . not so much praying as becoming a prayer." This integration of contemplation and action can be seen further in the common Franciscan saying, "The whole world is our cloister, brother body is our cell, and the soul is the hermit within." Just the same, in Jesus' prayer for His disciples, He calls us to live in the world without being caught up in the sins of the world (Jn. 17:15–18). Better yet, we are called to say with St. Paul, "For me, life is Christ" (Phil. 1:21; Gal. 2:20).

From this we can see that the stage of "daily life" for the Bride of Christ is a stage of deep mystical prayer and also a stage of highly practical and mundane apostolic activity. The activity is dry and lifeless without prayer, and the prayer becomes stifled if it does not naturally overflow into activity. It is truly a "mixed life" where contemplation and action are ideally synthesized into one.

Spiritual Parenting—Mothering and Fathering

This "mixed" stage is very much like being not only the Bride of Christ, but also the "mother" of the children that are born of that love union. As such, at this stage we all become "housewives" within mother Church.

We can see that Francis of Assisi was very much aware of this aspect of the Christian life. As we have read, Francis used the terminology of "mother" and "son" to describe the relationship between the brothers who lived in the prayerful solitude of the hermitages. Thomas of Celano speaks of the family attitude that should be engendered by this relationship in the hermitages saying, "Francis . . . admonished them to show to one another . . . the friendliness of family life. 'I wish,' he said, 'that my brothers would show themselves to be children of the same mother.'"

That Francis acted as that mother to his sons is seen in *The Mirror of Perfection* when his companions asked him what they shall do after he has died. "To whose charge will you leave us orphans? You have always been a father and mother to us; you have conceived and brought us forth in Christ. You have been our leader and shepherd, our instructor and corrector, teaching and correcting us by your example rather than by words."

This "motherhood" in Christ relates to our call to evangelize the world (Mt. 28:19). "Winning souls" for Christ is much like giving birth to new children in God's kingdom. Having been impregnated by the Spirit, we grow fat in the fruit of the Spirit as His divine seed matures in the womb of our life. When this spiritual pregnancy is complete, we naturally give birth to that new life within us. That new life is the newborn babe in Christ.

Many people try to force the delivery of this child before its time. This causes premature births and the many complications surrounding the special care needed to keep the premature baby alive. Even with our best efforts this premature baby sometimes dies.

Other people go to "prepared childbirth" classes to learn all about spiritual birthgiving when they have not yet been "impregnated" by the Spirit. They learn all the latest "how-to's" of evangelism, but without the impregnation of the Spirit these techniques are useless. It's no better than learning the breathing exercises used in natural childbirth. If you're not pregnant, you can pant till you're blue in the face; there still will be no baby! On the other hand, if a person has been impregnated by the Spirit, childbirth will occur even without the use of methods and techniques.

We know from experience that it can be very tough being a "housewife and a mother." The work is tiresome and thankless, often leaving one too drained to be a good wife when the husband does return and seeks the attention required for meaningful "love union." No matter how hard we try to enjoy our activity it still seems burdensome. Often we must leave the household to work in a different vineyard ourselves, and the burden seems doubled. Is it any wonder then that no matter how hard we try to prepare ourselves for the return of our Husband, all we really want to do is sleep?

The Difficult Times

At home or away, spiritually speaking, a common problem frequently arises called "spiritual dryness." The monks of the desert were well acquainted with it and sometimes called it the "noonday devil." During this stage we feel overworked and drained in our apostolic activity, yet when we attempt to pray we cannot find any living water. We look to scripture for a source of inspiration, but it all seems boring. Even the marvels of nature hold no wonder for us. We try to stir up our charismatic gifts and seek rapturous love union with Jesus, but it seems as if Jesus isn't interested anymore. Instead of love union between the Lover and the Beloved, prayer seems more like a sort of spiritual masturbation. Needless to say, instead of being able to find contemplative rest in the arms of our Lover, it seems we are forever sleeping alone. To put it quite simply, it seems as if the Jesus you once loved so much has suddenly vanished from your life.

Actually, Jesus has not deserted you at all; He is just helping to strengthen your love and faith. Remember, love is a decision. It is meant to include your feelings, but is not guided by feelings. As love matures it must become even more a decision if it is to endure.

Consider this: If love were based on feelings, marriages would never last. Our feelings can change like the wind and in most marriages they do, sometimes from one extreme to another. First we are excited, then we are bored. First we are infatuated, then we are disenchanted. First we love, then we come dangerously close to hate. At first we love to hear the voice of our lover, then even the sound of his voice bothers us. In the beginning we love to be in his presence, but later we can't wait for him to leave. Once we longed for his embrace and his kiss, but now we cannot even stand for him to touch us. In every marriage the romanticism of the relationship eventually wears thin. It is then that the substance of the marriage will be discovered and tested.

It is only a decision to love that will see the husband and wife through these tough times, and every marriage will have them sooner or later. A decision to love will hang in there even when the emotions border on hatred. A decision to love will remember the good times of the past and will faithfully look forward to the future. A de-

cision to love knows that if we continually fill our minds
with thoughts of love, soon the feeling of love will return
to our marriage (Rom. 12:2; Eph. 4:23), for where our
treasure lies there will our heart be also (Lk. 12:34).

This is not only a decision to love but also to have faith.
As we know, faith also involves the feelings, but is not
primarily guided by them. Faith is a decision, an act of
the will. The scriptures say that this faith is greater than
the things that are presently evident through sight and
feelings (2 Cor. 5:7; Rom. 8:24; Heb. 11:1). They also say
that faith will be tested through the feelings and experiences associated with trials and tribulations (1 Pt. 1:6–9).
Then faith and love will be truly strong and mature (James
1:2–4).

This is true also of our love relationship with Jesus. As
our relationship matures, times come when feelings of
love and faith seem to die. It is during these times of spiritual dryness that the real substance of our love and our
faith in Jesus will be tried and tested. Ironically, it is often
during these difficult times that our real spirituality grows
the most. As the parable of "Footprints in the Sand" illus-
trates, many times we can see Jesus' footprints alongside
of our own. But looking back to the hard times we sometimes only see one set of footprints in the sand. We often
think those are our own footprints and that during those
times Jesus had deserted us. But actually those are the
Lord's footprints, not ours, for He had been carrying us
when we were too weak to walk. So when we continue to
make a decision of love for Jesus, even when Jesus seems
to be gone, and even when our feelings of love seem to
have died, it is then that the spiritual substance of our
love relationship with Jesus really grows.

This whole process is alluded to in a previously men-
tioned story of Brother John of Alverna. First, Brother
John advanced quickly through the initial stages of love

relationship with Jesus. But later we see that John entered a time of spiritual dryness, not through sin, but by God's goodness! "But because God takes special care of His sons . . . it pleased God in His goodness to withdraw that light and fire of divine love from him and to deprive him of all spiritual consolations, leaving him without love or light and utterly miserable and depressed and mournful."

However, John did not commit the sin of self-pity or despair (2 Cor. 4:8). He responded by seeking God. "When his soul did not feel the presence of his Beloved, in his anguish and torment he went through the woods, running here and there, anxiously seeking and calling aloud with tears and sighs for his dear Friend who had recently left him and hidden, and without whose presence his soul could find no peace or rest. But nowhere and in no way could he find his Blessed Jesus Christ and enjoy as before the sweet spiritual consolations of His loving embraces.

"And he endured that trial for many days, mourning and sighing and weeping and praying God in His mercy to give him back the beloved Spouse of his soul."

Many people on the path to prayer have experienced the same thing. After having been wounded by mystical union with their Lover, they suddenly cannot find Him anywhere. But they do not give up in despair. They search for their Lover throughout the whole created world, and even then they cannot find Him.

Then something beautiful happens. Consider Brother John: "Finally, when it pleased God to have sufficiently tested his patience and inflamed his longing . . . our Blessed Lord Jesus Christ appeared on the path where Brother John had been walking, but He said nothing. . . . When Brother John saw Him and recognized Him, he immediately threw himself at His feet, and weeping uncontrollably he very humbly begged Him to help him. . . ."

The next section shows the reason for this divine game of holy hide-and-seek. "But because the longing of holy men increases to greater love and merit when God delays in granting its fulfillment, the Blessed Christ went away from him along the path. Then Brother John seeing that Christ was leaving without answering his prayer or saying anything to him, arose and ran after Him and again humbly threw himself at His feet, holding Him back with holy eagerness. Again the Savior went from him without saying anything to him or giving him any consolation." Jesus was acting like a mother with her baby who withdraws her breast from him to make him drink the milk more eagerly. After he cries and seeks it, she hugs and kisses him and lets him enjoy it all the more.

"So Brother John followed Christ a third time with greater fervor and desire, weeping like a baby following its mother . . . and when he came up to Him, the Blessed Christ turned toward him and looked at him with a joyful and loving expression on His face, and He held out and opened His holy and merciful arms. . . . And as He opened His arms, Brother John saw marvelous rays of light issuing from the holy breast of Christ. . . ."

After John had received an illumination of his soul from this light, "he felt completely renewed and pacified and consoled." Then, "Christ held out His most holy hands and opened them for him to kiss . . . and when he had kissed them, he came closer and leaned against the breast of Christ, and he embraced Jesus and kissed His holy bosom. And Christ likewise embraced and kissed him."

Summary

After having his faith and love thus tested, the Lover returned to the Beloved and filled Brother John with even greater spiritual gifts than before. In this wonderful Franciscan story we can see how the Lord gives us these times of spiritual dryness in order to test, strengthen, and actually increase the real lasting substance of our spirituality. This is the testing of the real spiritual substance of our personal love relationship with Jesus Christ.

We can conclude that this stage of "daily life" in the love relationship between the Lover and the Beloved is the most difficult and advanced stage of mysticism. It is the stage of a "mixed life" of contemplation and action that should be seen in all clerical and lay leaders, or mothers, within the Church. Involving the most advanced or mature apostolic activities of a parent raising children in the Church, the mystical prayer from which this activity bubbles forth must be very advanced and mature. We must know how to deal with times of spiritual consolation and times of spiritual dryness without ever compromising our decision to love our Husband through prayer or our children through service. This is a very difficult commitment, involving a high degree of maturity in both areas. That is why I place the stage of "daily life" toward the end of this book on the relationship between the Lover and the Beloved.

6

THE CROSS

✣

Having completed all the stages of the mystical love relationship between the Lover and the Beloved, there remains one element that must be an integral part of them all if this personal love relationship is to be fully Christian—the cross.

Many other religions have personalized manifestations of God, and some claim that God incarnated Himself in human form. All of these other incarnate gods teach wisdom, heal, and work awe-inspiring miracles. Likewise, the devotees of these religions are often invited to see their god as a lover and to enter into mystical love union with him as his bride. Even though it can be maintained that no other religion has as complete an incarnation of God as Christianity has in Jesus, there still remains an element of Jesus' ministry that makes our Lover unique among all religious expressions of the world—His cross.

Throughout the scriptures the cross is portrayed as an integral part of Jesus' ministry on earth. Jesus rebukes Peter for being an obstacle in His path to the cross for praying, "Heaven preserve you, Lord; this must not happen to you." Jesus then says, "The way you think is not God's way but man's" (Mt. 16:21–23). Jesus goes on to say of His incarnation and the way of the cross: "The Son of

Man came not to be served but to serve, and to give His life as a ransom for many" (Mt. 20:28). Again, in John's gospel He says it is for this reason that He came (Jn. 12: 23–28). He says that He must be lifted up on the cross (Jn. 3:13–14). Finally, Jesus says that the cross is the highest expression of God's love for his Beloved (Jn. 15:13; 10:11, 14–18).

Likewise, Jesus calls all of His followers to take up their own cross in the full manifestation of His gospel of love. After rebuking Peter for not understanding the way of the cross, He says, "If anyone wants to be a follower of mine, let him renounce himself and take up his cross and follow me" (Mt. 16:24–26). In speaking to the rich young ruler, Jesus says it is the unique way of the cross that will save him, even though he has known and practiced all the true riches of the Jewish religion (Mk. 10:21).

St. Paul preaches the gospel of Jesus Christ by proclaiming the uniqueness of the cross as "God's power to save" (1 Cor. 1:17–18). To the Galatians, Paul admits that this preaching seems scandalous to other religions (Gal. 5:11). Yet he says that not only will he boast only in the preaching of the cross, but that the cross is the final religious "rule" for God's true people (Gal. 6:14–16).

So the cross must be manifested and experienced in the various stages of our personal love relationship with Jesus Christ if this mystical encounter is to be fully Christian. If, in our mystical experiences, we have not yet reached the perfection of the cross, then we have not yet gone far enough. However, if we think we have gone beyond the foolishness of the cross, we have gone too far and have not yet begun the mystical love encounter at all. It is the foolishness of the cross of Jesus that reveals all of the mysteries of God and unites the Lover to His Bride on earth (Col. 1:19–20).

Discipline

The way of the cross can be followed in the first, or "dialogue," stage in our relationship with Jesus, our divine Lover, by developing a disciplined program of study and meditation, and sticking to it even when we might feel like doing something else.

A similar situation exists with a husband and wife. In today's busy world, unless a couple sets aside special times for dialogue in uninhibited honesty, they often will never get around to this much-needed dimension of a healthy marriage. Without frequent and regular times for open and honest communication, even the best of marriages will fail. Yet in today's world these times must be planned and set aside, or else the busy whirlwind of normal family activities will sweep the opportunities away. Most successful Christian marriage programs strongly recommend the discipline of regularly scheduled dialogue times for a husband and wife.

Keeping this discipline is not an easy thing to do. The myriad possible activities present in normal family life will often seem to be just so many good reasons to cancel this "appointment" between the husband and wife. Yet canceling or postponing this time will only set an unhealthy precedent for the whole mindset of the family, which will push this precious time of dialogue to the bottom of the priority list, somewhere after making popcorn together. In short, the dialogue will seldom occur. In the long run this can destroy the quality of a marriage, a family, and a home, and inflict the wound of separation and divorce into the living flesh of an entire family.

The same thing holds true for the relationship between the Lover and the Beloved in the family of Christ. We must set aside daily times for dialogue with Jesus through study and meditation, or else our relationship could die.

We should faithfully keep a daily schedule for meditation. This time should also be at the top of our list of priorities, kept as a "sacred time" which remains virtually unmoved by the normal flow of daily activities.

It will be difficult to keep this meditation time once you have committed to a daily horarium. Once you set the time aside a thousand "good" reasons to move or cancel the meditation time will rush in on you. But don't do it. This time is very important to the health and quality of your relationship with Jesus. This time is sacred.

The Book of Sirach speaks of the discipline needed to cultivate wisdom in a similar way. There is hard work involved, but it promises even greater rewards:

> *My son, from your youth*
> *embrace discipline;*
> *thus will you find wisdom*
> *with graying hair,*
> *for in cultivating her you will*
> *labor but little,*
> *and soon you will eat*
> *of her fruits.*
> (Sir. 6:18–20)

Later, the author speaks of discipline in a way that is reminiscent of the cross and resurrection of Christ saying,

> *Put your feet into her fetters*
> *and your neck under her yoke.*
> *Stoop your shoulders and carry her;*
> *and be not irked at her bonds.*
> *Thus will you afterward find*
> *rest in her,*
> *and she will become your joy.*

Her fetters will be your throne
of majesty;
her bonds, your purple cord.
(Sir. 6:25–30)

We cannot help but be reminded of the words of Jesus who also alludes to the paradox of the cross saying, "Come to Me, all you who are weary and find life burdensome, and I will refresh you. Take my yoke upon your shoulders and learn from me, for I am gentle and humble of heart. Your souls will find rest, for my yoke is easy and my burden light" (Mt. 12:28–30).

From these scriptures we can conclude that to embrace the cross of a disciplined study and meditation schedule will yield in time to new life. If we stoop our shoulders under the cross now, in time of trouble and weakness this cross will hold us up straight and tall.

All of the Franciscan spiritual masters urged the serious student of Christian meditation to embrace the cross of a daily schedule or discipline. Francis himself kept a personal discipline even when traveling. "When he went through the world on foot, he always stopped to say the hours; when he was on horseback, he got down upon the ground.... He used to say at times 'If the body takes its food in quiet ... with what great peace and tranquility should not the soul take its food, which is God Himself.'" The liturgical hours of the Church are, in fact, prayed at certain times every day. But Francis put such a high priority on maintaining a scheduled time for dialogue with Jesus through prayer and meditation that he willingly fought for this privilege in the midst of a busy schedule. Furthermore to insure a quality environment for this prayer, he totally stopped what he was doing and gave his full attention to his meditation. No doubt this was often difficult for Francis to maintain, but from all

biographical indications he faithfully embraced this cross
and kept the promise to go aside for awhile and speak to
his Love (Hos. 2:16).

Asceticism

Beyond setting aside time, there is another discipline
involved in setting a proper environment for dialogue and
love union. For a couple in love, setting is very important. It should be quiet, free from noisy phone calls and
unexpected knocks on the door. And if dialogue is to begin over a romantic, candlelit dinner, the sensitive lover
won't grab a Big Mac and shake an hour before the meal
starts! You want it to be special and memorable. You
want your mind clear of clutter as well, especially when
there is a delicate issue to be discussed, because it is important to be able to focus your entire attention on the
words of the one you love. In all these things the lover
does with less temporarily, so that in the long run dialogue and love union might be more fully appreciated,
shared, and accomplished between lover and beloved. A
bombardment of sensual pleasures too quickly and at one
time dulls the senses, whereas a careful course of small
delights will heighten awareness and appreciation. Less is
more, and the careful moderation of the senses creates an
environment in which love might be sensitively received
and given as you move toward union.

The same is true in our relationship with Christ. Not
only do we need to set aside special times, but we also
need to set aside special places and to establish certain attitudes for our spiritual dialogue and encounter to succeed. An attitude of silence and solitude will sensitize us
for an intimate encounter with the living Word. If we silence our senses through fasting and self-denial, we will
purge them of the selfishness and lust that dulls us; the

perceptions of our hearts will be highly attuned as we receive the living Bread. When the senses of the body are kept "in solitude" and not overindulged, they will be more sensitive to the subtle working of the Spirit. Through these acts of self-denial the spiritual senses rise to a sharper, higher level of perception. Therefore in silence we find the Word, in solitude our Companion. In fasting we come to savor the Bread of Life and our Cup of Salvation. Without the ascesis of moderation we could easily pass over the subtle and delicate beauties of the eternal Spirit and settle for the short-lived gratifications of the flesh.

In this healthy asceticism the cross must be embraced if we are to make it through to the resurrection. It is hard to be silent when the world screams for a constant reply, to be solitary when the business of this world constantly knocks at your door. It is hard to fast in prayer when the world constantly requests the honor of your presence at the newest restaurant. Even the American Church calls her members to an endless maze of Church socials and pot-luck dinners! To these we must learn to say an occasional no.

Your flesh will cry out in apparent agony, but it is being deceived. It will not die if its appetites are moderated. Its appetites will rise again in God's beauty rather than in the masquerade of an artificial and misguided humanity. Surprisingly, if we learn the art of the occasional no, we will come to appreciate more fully both God and human companionship, the spoken word, and the holy meal that binds families and communities together as around the sacred altar of Christ.

Sacrifice

The discipline of asceticism is also a positive way to move beyond dialogue into touching the Crucified with your whole soul and body as well as spirit. True asceticism is not a denial of the physical world; it affirms the reality and goodness of all God's creation. True asceticism is a healthy, wholistic response to Jesus Christ, rather than an imbalanced response that views the created world of flesh and blood as evil. It is the positive love-response of the Bride as she reaches out to share the sufferings of her Groom.

But how? How can the human body reach out and actually touch the incarnate Christ Jesus on the cross? We can by identifying with our Lover through fastings, vigils, silence, and solitude. Fasting not only moderates our often uncontrolled appetites, it also brings us into love union with Jesus in the desert of His temptations and in the tribulation of His cross where He was offered only sour wine and vinegar to drink. Vigils not only curb our laziness and unhealthy desire for sleep, they also bring us into intimate union with Jesus during His vigil at Gethsemani and His mock midnight trial before the Sanhedrin and later before Pontius Pilate. Silence not only checks our tendency to uncontrolled speech, it brings us into communion with the One who was silent before His accusers with the meekness and humility of a lamb. In all these, the cross of self-denial is embraced out of love, not out of law. All these physical disciplines become ways to unite our bodies as well as our spirits to our Lover, Christ Crucified.

The same idea is suggested by Francis's espousal of Lady Poverty. Born naked in a shepherd's stable at Bethlehem and crucified with thieves, hanging naked upon a cross on Calvary, Christ Himself was the first to take Lady Poverty as His Bride. I believe Francis sought not only to imitate Christ, but to touch the poor Christ as he reached out to hold and honor Jesus' Lady Poverty through the austerities of his own life. Solitary vigils, fastings, and itinerant wanderings all provided the means through which he could embrace the poor incarnate Christ, his divine Lover and his humble Lord.

The cross must therefore be embraced in the second stage of the relationship between the Lover and the Beloved. In this stage the Bride must totally sacrifice her body by embracing the cross of Christ for the sake of her Husband, who has also totally sacrificed His body on the cross of Calvary for the sake of His Bride. In this mutual sacrifice of love the two become one as this mystical marriage is consummated in the passion of the cross. As the two totally die to self in giving for the other, new life is born in the one Body of Christ.

St. John of the Cross speaks of the consummation of our spiritual marriage with Jesus as taking place in the embrace of the cross. In *The Living Flame of Love* he writes:

> *O living flame of love*
> *That tenderly wounds my soul*
> *In its deepest center! Since*
> *Now you are not oppressive,*
> *Now consumate! If it be your will:*
> *Tear through the veil of this*
> *sweet encounter!*
> *O sweet cautery*
> *O delightful wound!*
> *O gentle hand! O delicate touch*
> *That tastes of eternal life*
> *And pays every debt!*
> *In killing You changed death to life.*

This spiritual sexuality stands in total contrast to the sexuality of the world. Most of the sexuality of this world seeks the passion of intercourse with a spouse for the sake of self-fulfillment. Many times the moment of climax and union is a moment lusted after for the sake of the self. Selfishness and lust are often the driving forces behind the sexuality of the world. This is why most of today's sexuality is, in fact, ungodly, immoral, and sinful.

The sexuality of the Lover and the Beloved is something entirely different. It is something sacred and holy. This is because we seek this mystical union totally for the sake of our divine Lover, just as He sought only the fulfillment of His Beloved on Calvary. At the moment of spiritual climax, or rapture, we seek only to fulfill our Lover, Jesus Christ. The world's lovers seek and lust after the fulfillment of the self, often to the detriment of their spouse. The Lover and the Beloved seek only the fulfillment of the other, totally abandoning themselves for the benefit of the other, coming together in a spiritual climax that is consequently mutually and totally self-fulfilling without even the slightest stain of ungodliness or lust.

This is not to say there is no passion in this mystical union. On the contrary, the story of Jesus' embrace of the cross of Calvary is, in fact, called the Passion. It was with much human and divine love and emotion that Jesus gave His life for the sake of His Bride. He cried many tears and sweat drops of blood in the anguish and suffering of the cross. Yet even in the midst of this pain He no doubt remembered His own words to the crowds which assured that His "yoke is easy" and His "burden is light." There was no anger or resentment in this pain, for Jesus' love for His Bride turned the bitterness of death into a sweet suffering. It was in the sweetness of this suffering that He could painfully cry out not only, "My God, my God, why have You forsaken me," but also in forgiving love, "Father, forgive them; they do not know what they are doing."

So it is as the Bride takes up and embraces her cross every day. She will experience much human and divine passion as she embraces the cross and her mystical marriage to the Bridegroom is consummated. It will be an experience of much emotion and passion. She will experience all the joy and the pain, the unswerving faith and the confusion, the fulfilling comfort and the suffering that her Lover experienced on the cross. Through all this a sweetness will endure that will fulfill her even in the midst of any pain. Here we are reminded of St. Stephen who, like his Lover before him, forgave his executioners because of the fullness of love felt even in the midst of a painful death (Acts 7:54–60). So with the Bride. To the degree that she abandons herself to the cross of this mystical and consummating union, she will be fulfilled.

So the awesome paradox of the cross is in this mystical union. The more we die to our self, the more our self will be fulfilled. The more we seek nothing at all from this spiritual intercourse, the more we will taste total fulfillment. The more we seek only to die in the consummation of this mystical marriage, the more we will find new life within the womb of our spiritual body. So it is that the lifting up of Jesus on the cross of humiliation and death reveals both God's salvation and glory (Jn. 3:14; 8:28; 12:32).

This is graphically illustrated in the accounts of the stigmata of St. Francis, when he miraculously received the marks of Christ crucified in his hands, feet, and side. Of this event, St. Bonaventure says, "It was set before his eyes, that, as Christ's lover, he might know he was to resemble Christ crucified perfectly.... One morning about the feast of the Exaltation of the Holy Cross, as he was praying on the mountainside, Francis saw a Seraph with six fiery wings coming down from the highest point in heaven.... He saw that the Seraph was nailed to a Cross although he had wings....

"Francis was dumbfounded at the sight and his heart was flooded with a mixture of joy and sorrow. He was overjoyed to see how graciously Christ regarded him .... But the sight of the cruel way he was nailed to the cross pierced his soul with a sword of compassionate sorrow.... As the vision disappeared it left his heart ablaze with seraphic eagerness and marked his body with the visible likeness of the Crucified."

Here we see many of the elements we have discussed coming together in the stigmata of Francis of Assisi. He knows Jesus as his Lover in direct connection to the experience of the mystery of the cross. He tastes the passion of the cross in a wide variety of conflicting emotions. A "new wine" intoxicates him with new and eternal life in this spiritual intercourse, yet the experience leaves his body marked with the marks of Jesus' death.

Clearly, Francis's stigmata was seen as the love-touch of the Beloved. "His soul melted when his beloved spoke to him. A little later, the love of his heart made itself manifest by the wounds of his body."

That Francis's devotion to the cross was always tender, compassionate, and full of that bittersweetness promised him at his conversion is evident in every story known about him. "The entire public and private life of the man of God," writes Celano, "centered about the cross of the Lord; and from the first moment when he became a knight of the Crucified, various mysteries of the cross shone forth in him." The *Legend of Perugia* says that when Francis meditated on the passion and humility of Christ, "he experienced much compassion and much sweetness from this, and in the end, what was bitter to his body was changed into sweetness." Celano says that in receiving the stigmata, Francis was both "sorrowful and joyful, and joy and grief were in him alternately." The *Mirror of Perfection* tells how Francis would pick up a stick from the ground and use it as though he were playing a violin and would joyfully dance and sing in French of Jesus. "But all this jollity would end in tears, and his joy would melt away in compassion for the sufferings of Christ."

From all this we can see that Francis experienced the cross as a passionate consummation of his mystical marriage with Jesus.

We might rightfully respond that this mystical experience is fine and good for Francis, since he also had the intense experience of bearing the stigmata, but such an experience of mystical union is far beyond the reach of us normal Christians. After all, such extraordinary manifestations are bound to bring an extraordinary internal spiritual union with Jesus, aren't they?

But let us remember that Francis bore the stigmata in his heart long before he bore them on his body. From the time of his conversion, claims *The Legend of the Three Companions*, "his heart was stricken and wounded with melting love and compassion for the passion of Christ; and for the rest of his life he carried in it the wounds of the Lord Jesus." Francis's stigmata were only an external manifestation of what had long been an internal reality in his life.

In this we can see that all of us are called to bear the stigmata of Jesus' cross on our hearts. Few if any of us will ever bear the miraculous stigmata on our body, except for the normal consequences of our living the gospel spoken of by St. Paul (Gal. 6:17). Yet all of us are called to bear the marks of the Lord on our heart in the same passionate way St. Francis did. Let us conclude, then, that the passionate love touch of Jesus crucified is the consummating act of our spiritual marriage with the Lord.

Being

The cross must also be embraced as we enter the third stage of our love relationship with Jesus, the Bridegroom of our soul. In this stage all intellectual speculation and all emotional passion must die as we learn how to simply be with Christ. We will experience an intellectual death when scripture study and spiritual reading no longer interest or challenge. We will experience an emotional death when the excitement of charismatic rapture and ecstasy cease to occur every time we pray or even frequently. We will experience a death when we wonder if we have done something wrong in our spiritual life, or even if God has abandoned us.

But as we have said before, Jesus is just taking us through the cross in a temporary death to both "dialogue," or study and meditation, and "love union," or charismatic rapture and ecstasy. If we simply relax and enter willingly into this "wound of love," then we will find a resurrection as we enter into the stage of "afterglow," or true contemplative prayer. This is, however, a very confusing time for many, and involves a definite experience of the cross as we let go of the familiar and comfortable former stages and advance to contemplative maturity in our relationship with Jesus (Heb. 6:1).

St. Bonaventure speaks of the cross as being an essential part of crossing over into this contemplative stage of our relationship with Jesus. Toward the end of *The Journey of the Mind to God* he says, "It now remains for the soul ... to transcend and go beyond not only this sensible world, but even its own self. In this going beyond, Christ is the way and the door, Christ is the ladder and the conveyance, the propitiatory ... placed over the Ark of God....

"Whoever looks upon the propitiatory and turns his face fully toward the Crucified ... makes the ... passover in the company of Christ. By the staff of the cross, he enters the Red Sea, on his way out of Egypt to the desert; there he tastes the hidden manna, and with Christ he lies in the tomb, apparently dead to the world, but all the while experiencing in himself ... what was said on the cross to the robber who confessed Christ, 'Amen, I say to thee, this day thou shalt be with me in paradise'" (Lk. 23:43). Here we have only to remember that the mystical tradition of Christianity often speaks of the desert as being a symbol of the contemplative life, and the tomb as becoming the womb from which new spiritual life is conceived and brought forth.

Bonaventure then goes on to speak of the stigmata of Francis as an invitation to all people to embrace the cross of Jesus in this passing over into the contemplative life. "This was shown likewise to blessed Francis on the height of the mountain (where I thought out the things I have written here) when, in a rapture of contemplation, he had a vision of a six-winged Seraph attached to a Cross . . . . There, carried out of himself, he passed over to God, becoming a perfect model of contemplation . . . so that,in this way and through him, God might invite all truly spiritual men, rather by example than by word, to the same passing over . . . .

"If this passing over is to be perfect, all intellectual operations must be given up, and the sharp point of our desire must be . . . transformed in Him. . . . Let us die, then, and pass over into the darkness; let us silence every care, every craving, every dream; with Christ crucified let us 'pass out of this world to the Father'" (Jn. 13:1).

Here Bonaventure brings out the natural flow from experiencing the cross in the passionate consummation of our mystical marriage to experiencing the cross in the contemplative afterglow with Jesus. Ideally, one flows from the other, so that if we relax and flow with the rhythm of the Spirit we will move from one stage almost unnoticeably into the other. Thus, we are led by the Spirit into the desert with Jesus (Lk. 4:1) where we experience the cross that leads us to the rich aridity of wordless and imageless prayer.

It is only when we fight this move of the Spirit that we

experience an unnecessary crucifixion and pain that is bitter. As he says, "Such a motion as this is something mystical and very secret, and no one knows it . . . unless the fire of the Holy Spirit . . . inflames him to the very marrow. That is why the apostle attributes to the Holy Spirit the revelation of such mystical wisdom."

Even having said this, it is clear that Bonaventure sees the sweet pain of the cross as the necessary doorway of Christ through which we pass over into the stage of contemplative "afterglow." It is the cross of Jesus that makes Francis of Assisi "the perfect model of contemplation." It is the cross that leads us into the divine darkness, silencing "every care, every craving, every dream." It is the cross that causes us to "pass out of this world to the Father." So it is the cross that leads us to the "afterglow" where we can say with Bonaventure: "Nothing more is to come but the day of quiet, on which . . . the human mind rests after all its labors."

Contemplation and Action

Finally, the cross is experienced in the fourth stage of "daily life" within the family of Jesus Christ. It is in this last stage that all the previous stages converge, so that the cross is experienced more intensely here than in any previous stage of relationship with Christ. It is as if this stage is a combination and a microcosm of all the other stages, intensifying the experience of the cross for the Bride of Christ as the other of many children within the Church.

Needless to say, the crosses of this "mixed life" are many. The main cross has to do with the creative tension between contemplation and action in this mixed life. While the pool of contemplative prayer flows out naturally into active work like streams in the desert, during the period of activity you will always long and yearn to return to the source of contemplative prayer. This tension is part and parcel of a "mixed life" and should not be viewed as an indication that something is wrong. In fact, it is this creative tension between contemplation and action that gives added power to both.

It is much like the creative tension on the string of a high-powered bow. Without this tension the bow cannot properly shoot the arrow sure and straight into the target. If there is too much tension on the string, it will snap, leaving the bow unable to shoot at all. There must be a proper balance between contemplation and action in order for our tension to remain creative. Yet even when this tension is creative and good, it remains a cross for us as we long to share the gospel from our contemplation, and yearn to return to contemplation during our active ministry.

The further crosses are simply inherent in the hard work of activity of ministering to this "family of God." Think of the priests and ministers who spend their lives proclaiming the gospel of Jesus and ministering the sacraments in faraway places. Think of the husbands and wives who labor tirelessly in sacrificing with Christ their whole life for the sake of their families. Most of this work is taken for granted and goes virtually unnoticed. There are few words of gratitude and thanks to keep them going through the many times of discouragement. This is, indeed, a great cross for these brave souls to bear.

As we have determined before, this "mixed life" is by its nature a life of Christian leadership. The spiritual maturity required of this last stage in our relationship with Christ puts everyone into a position of formal or informal leadership within the Church. They may not consider themselves to be leaders in the formal sense of the word, but even their humble example will serve both to birth and to raise spiritual children in Christ.

As such, St. Bonaventure's work on Christian leadership,

The Six Wings of the Seraph, can be applied to almost anyone who has entered into the stage of this mixed life. In this work we hear him speak of the maturity required of those who do not need a master but teach others through word and deed.

St. Bonaventure speaks of the patience needed to bear the cross during this leadership when he says, "A superior is much in need of patience because of the slow progress of those for whom he is laboring. He sees . . . that few are advancing; he sees that his work is almost wasted, as a man who sows much but sees little grow.

"A superior needs patience to cope with the ingratitude of those for whom he is laboring with such loving care. Hardly ever satisfied, they always complain that he could treat them differently and better if he only wanted to. . . . They distort most of what he does and misinterpret it. Hence, they bother him; they complain, accuse, criticize; and find cause for scandal in the very things by which he thought he was serving both God and them. Hardly is he able to take any remedial step without his command or action displeasing or upsetting someone."

Surely such a description involves the experience of the cross! Bonaventure says further that the leader should respond to these hardships with "the shield of threefold patience," which in itself implies a certain death to self. "First, let him answer every criticism humbly, maturely, and kindly, containing his ardor so as not to reveal any impatience in his voice, expression, or attitude. Being patient, he will better succeed. . . . Second, let him try to be peaceful by not taking revenge on personal affronts, and by bearing in his heart no hatred against offenders. His concern for their welfare should not diminish, nor should he try to get rid of them. . . . Third, he should be long-suffering so that the exhaustion of heavy work, the slowness of his subjects' progress, and the irritations and troubles they procure may have no detrimental effect on his will or effort to do all that is needed for the faithful accomplishment of his task."

He then goes on to speak of the benefit these crosses bring to the leader's own spiritual life. "By such trials a superior is cleansed of the dust of sin he gathers.... The very number of a superior's duties is the occasion of many failings of which he should cleanse himself in this world so as not to be more severely punished in the next.... Furthermore, while the superior is afflicted by these trials, he is saved from the swelling of pride. The loftiness of a superior's position, the extent of his freedom, and possible conceit over his good works, would easily make him proud, were it not for the yoke of adversity that bends the neck of his presumption, and thus saves him from the abyss of pride."

Bonaventure then speaks of the merit that is stored up for the leader without him even knowing it, so complete is his experience of his cross. "A superior's merit will increase not only with the glory he acquires by furthering good in himself and others, but also through the magnificent crown he receives for bearing adversities.... Oftentimes spiritual life becomes more intense without revealing its growth, and is strengthened most when it seems to be weakening."

Francis of Assisi experienced so many trials and crosses during his time of leadership that he eventually resigned his office and took up the simple life of an obedient brother. It is not difficult to sense Francis's frustration in the *Mirror of Perfection*: "Once, when asked by one of the friars why he had abandoned his charge of the friars ... he replied, 'My son, I love the brethren to the utmost of my power, but if they would follow my footsteps I would love them still more, and would not make myself a stranger to them. For some of the superiors pull them in another direction, holding up to them as patterns the men of long ago, and disregarding my warnings . . . .'

"And shortly afterwards, when he was burdened with severe illness, he raised himself in bed, and cried out in vehemence of spirit, "Who are these who have torn my Order and my friars out of my hands? If I come to the General Chapter I will make my intention clear.'"

These words communicate the pain inflicted upon him by the very community he birthed. The same friars who, as his spiritual children, called him "mother" and "father" were the very instruments used to bring the greatest cross into the life of Francis. This has led many to speculate that the physical stigmata he received during his solitary sojourn in the hermitage on Mt. Alverna came primarily as a result of the cross he bore in his heart inflicted by the very community he founded.

From all of this we can conclude that the cross must be an important part of every stage in our love relationship with Jesus, if this mystical experience is to be fully Christian. In every day of our life we must take up our cross and follow the Lord. We must embrace the cross of disciplined meditation and study if our relationship with Jesus is to be fully guided by truth. We must passionately embrace the cross of total abandonment and giving of self in the charismatic rapture of the consummation of our mystical marriage. We must accept the cross of the silencing of our intellect and our feelings in the contemplative "afterglow" of simply being with Jesus. Finally, we must embrace the cross of "daily life" with Jesus, as we experience the mix of contemplation and action that brings us face to face with the challenge. Yet if we embrace the cross in all the stages, we will find a new life in Christ that will truly prove that His yoke is easy and His burden is light.

It would not be fitting to conclude this chapter without

recalling the wonderful story which best depicts Francis's intense love of the cross. The *Little Flowers* tells us that one day Francis and Brother Leo were coming to St. Mary of the Angels from Perugia suffering keenly from the bitter cold. "St. Francis called to Brother Leo . . . and said, 'Brother Leo, even if the Friars Minor in every country give a great example of holiness and integrity and good edification, nevertheless write down and note carefully that perfect joy is not in that.'

"And when they had walked a bit, St. Francis called him again, saying: 'Brother Leo, even if a Friar Minor gives sight to the blind, heals the paralyzed, drives out devils, gives hearing back to the deaf, makes the lame walk, and restores speech to the dumb, and what is still more, brings back to life a man who has been dead four days, write that perfect joy is not in that.'

"And going on a bit, St. Francis cried out again in a strong voice: 'Brother Leo, if a Friar Minor knew all languages and all sciences and Scripture, if he also knew how to prophesy and reveal not only the future but also the secrets of the consciences and minds of others, write down and note carefully that perfect joy is not in that.'

"And as they walked on, after a while St. Francis called again forcefully: 'Brother Leo, little Lamb of God, even if a Friar Minor could speak with the voice of an angel, and know the courses of the stars and the powers of the herbs, and knew all about the treasures in the earth, and if he knew the qualities of birds and fishes, animals, humans, roots, trees, rocks and waters, write down and note carefully that true joy is not in that.'

"And going on a bit further, St. Francis called again strongly: 'Brother Leo, even if a Friar Minor could preach so well that he should convert all infidels to the faith of Christ, write that perfect joy is not there.'

"Now when he had been talking this way for a distance

of two miles, Brother Leo in great amazement asked him:
'Father, I beg you in God's name to tell me where perfect
joy is.'

"And St. Francis replied: 'When we come to St. Mary
of the Angels, soaked with the rain and frozen by the cold,
all soiled with mud and suffering from hunger, and we
ring the gate of the Place and the brother porter comes
and says angrily: 'Who are you?' And we say: 'We are
two of your brothers.' And he contradicts us, saying: 'You
are not telling the truth. Rather you are two rascals who
go around deceiving people and stealing what they give
to the poor. Go away!' And he does not open for us, but
makes us stand outside in the snow and rain, cold and
hungry, until night falls—then if we endure all those insults and cruel rebuffs patiently, without being troubled
and without complaining, and if we reflect charitably that
that porter really knows us and that God makes him speak
against us, oh, Brother Leo, write that perfect joy is there!

"'And if we continue to knock, and the porter comes
out in anger, and drives us away with curses and hard
blows like bothersome scoundrels, saying: 'Get away
from here, you dirty thieves—go to the hospital! Who do
you think you are? You certainly won't eat or sleep here!'—
and if we bear it patiently and take the insults with joy
and love in our hearts, oh, Brother Leo, write that that is
perfect joy!

"'And if later, suffering intensely from hunger and the
painful cold, with night falling, we still knock and call,
and crying loudly beg them to open for us and let us come
in for the love of God, and he grows still more angry and
says: 'Those fellows are bold and shameless ruffians. I'll
give them what they deserve!' And he comes out with a
knotty club and grasping us by the cowl throws us onto
the ground, rolling us in the mud and snow, and beats us
with that club so much that he covers us with wounds—if

we endure all those evils and insults and blows with joy and patience, reflecting that we must accept and bear the sufferings of the Blessed Christ patiently for love of Him, oh, Brother Leo, write: that is perfect joy!

" 'And now hear the conclusion, Brother Leo. Above all the graces and gifts of the Holy Spirit which Christ gives to His friends is that of conquering oneself and willingly enduring sufferings, insults, humiliations, and hardship for the love of Christ. For we cannot glory in all those other marvelous gifts of God, as they are not ours but God's, as the Apostle says, 'What have you that you have not received?'

" 'But we can glory in the Cross of tribulations and afflictions, because that is ours, and so the Apostle says, 'I will not glory save in the Cross of our Lord Jesus Christ!'

"To whom be honor and glory forever and ever. Amen."

From this one story about Francis's understanding of perfect joy we can see every stage of our relationship with Jesus spoken of as imperfect without inclusion of the cross. "Dialogue," which includes great knowledge and study and meditation of all the creation and the scriptures, is imperfect compared to the perfection of the cross. "Love union," which includes all the charismatic gifts and mystical graces, is imperfect compared to the cross. "Afterglow," which includes all the so-called perfection of the contemplative life, is really imperfect compared to the cross. "Daily life," which includes all the mature ministries and labors of evangelizing through example and word, is imperfect without a keen understanding of the cross.

In this story, Francis includes more wonderful accomplishments than most of us could ever imagine or experience, yet he also describes an experience of the cross that is far beyond most of us. Actually, the story of perfect joy calls us all to grow in both areas. It calls us to expand in all the accomplishments that we have studied in the stages of our love relationship with Jesus Christ. Yet, it especially calls us to grow in our understanding and experience of the cross. If we grow in the cross, we will find that we will also grow in progress through the various stages. Likewise, if we really progress through the stages, we can only do so by embracing the cross.

We can look to Francis as a good example. Francis was a nature mystic and a man of scripture. Francis was a Spirit-filled charismatic in the fullest sense of the word. Francis was an ideal model for the contemplative. Francis was a great evangelizer and a founder of many communities. Yet the only reason Francis was any of these things is that he was first and foremost a man of the cross. Beloved Francis was, more than anything else, the bearer of the marks of the Lover—Jesus crucified.

Conclusion

This concludes our look into the stages of progress in the mystical love relationship between the Lover and the Beloved. I have shared only what my own experience and knowledge as a young Franciscan hermit-troubadour can reveal. Know that the works from which I have quoted all speak with much more authority and detail on this sacred subject. Looking back on this, my feeble attempt to express the inexpressible, I can now only direct you on to the real spiritual masters of our rich and beautiful Christian tradition. In speaking of so delicate and beautiful a subject, as the mystical love relationship between the Lover and the Beloved, I must admit that I feel like a nervous bride on her wedding night trying to give the precious gift of herself to her husband, yet not really knowing how. I can only pray that this candid sharing of my own relationship with Jesus will, in some way, inspire you on to even greater mystical heights in your own relationship with this divine Lover.

Yet let me leave one final word of caution. In looking back over these stages, realize that, as you mature, all of them might be experienced again and again. Sometimes the stages will even seem to occur simultaneously as they charismatically ebb and flow in and out of one another in the rhythm of the Holy Spirit. You will not pass from one to the other, leaving the previous stages forever behind you. Even the most advanced contemplative will continue to study and meditate on scripture; nor will he spurn any shower of charismatic gifts that his Lover wishes to bestow. Those who think that they have advanced beyond these so-called "childish" things only reveal that they have not yet begun their own personal love relationship with Jesus Christ, who desires all to approach Him as little children. Are we too advanced for this? Perhaps we have not yet been spiritually reborn.

Finally, let these stages that I have written about with ink and paper move beyond the written word and become a living reality in your life. Our love relationship with Jesus must be fully alive! To limit the dynamics of divine love to the legalism of a method or a form is to take the very life from them. Jesus gives us this love so that we might have life and have it to the full (Jn. 10:10).

So let Jesus touch you and know you with the Holy Spirit. With Bonaventure and the Franciscan mystics, let Him inflame your heart to its very marrow. With John of the Cross, let the divine Lover come and touch your life with His living flame of love. With the seraphic fool of love, Francis of Assisi, let Him stigmatize your heart so that you might live in the sacred wounds of love forever. Then you will move beyond these feeble, earthly words of mine and enter into the heavenly marriage supper of the Lamb. Then will you enter the very nuptial chamber of this mystical marriage between the Lover and the Beloved.

RECOMMENDED READING

✤

The following list of books includes many of those quoted throughout this work as well as others that treat various aspects of Franciscan prayer.

Bernard of Clairvaux, St. *On the Song of Songs.* Edited by E. Rozanne Elder. Kalamazoo, Cistercian Publications, Inc., 1971.

Bonaventure, St. *The Works of Bonaventure.* Edited by P. Glorieux. Clifton, N.J.: St. Anthony's Guild, 1960.

Francis and Clare: The Complete Works. Edited by Regis J. Armstrong and Ignatius C. Brady. Ramsey, N.J.: Paulist Press, 1983.

Habig, Marion A., ed. *Omnibus of Sources.* Chicago: Franciscan Herald Press, 1983.

John of the Cross, St. *The Collected Works.* Translated by Kieran Kavanaugh and Otilio Rodriguez. Washington, D.C.: ICS Publications, 1964.

Johnston, William, ed. *The Cloud of Unknowing.* New York: Doubleday & Co., 1973.

Maes, Bonface. *Franciscan Mysticism.* Translated by Dom Basil Whelan. Pulaski, Wis.: Franciscan Publishers, 1956.

Peter of Alcantara, St. *A Golden Treatise of Mental Prayer.* Edited by G. S. Hollings. Chicago: Franciscan Herald Press, 1978.

Wroblewski, Sergius. *Bonaventurian Theology of Prayer.* Pulaski, Wis.: Franciscan Publishers, 1967.